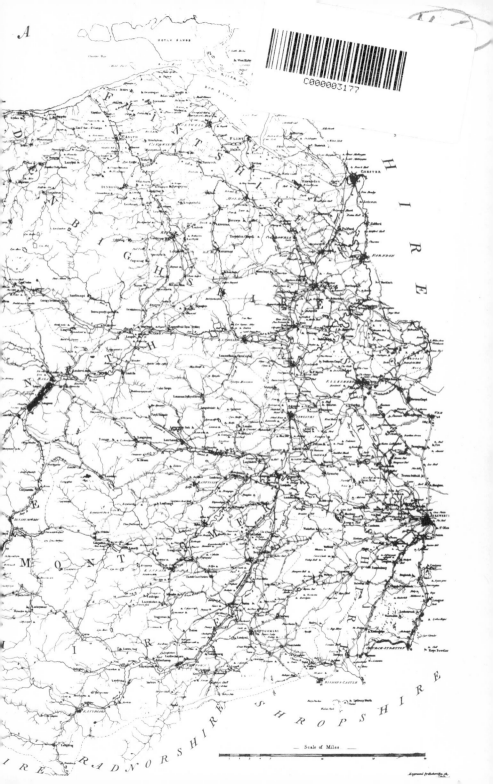

Scale of Miles

A Pedestrian Tour
through
North Wales,
in a Series of Letters

Joseph Hucks at Eton (1790), by Richard Livesay.

A Pedestrian Tour through North Wales, in a Series of Letters

by

J. Hucks, B.A.

(1795)

Edited by
Alun R. Jones
and
William Tydeman

Cardiff
University of Wales Press
1979

© Alun R. Jones and William Tydeman, 1979

British Library Cataloguing in Publication Data

Hucks, J.
  A pedestrian tour through North Wales, in a series
  of letters.
  1. Wales, North – Description and travel
  2. Wales, North – Correspondence
  I. Title   II. Jones, Alun Richard   III. Tydeman, William
  914.29'1'0473   DA740.N6

  ISBN 0–7083–0703–5

Text set in 10/11 pt VIP Plantin, printed and bound
in Great Britain at The Pitman Press, Bath

Contents

List of Illustrations

Endpapers: Map of North Wales (1797) by J. Evans, a reduced version of his large-scale map, issued in nine sheets during 1794–5. Visiting Wales too early to make use of Evans's maps, Hucks and Coleridge probably carried a popular pocket atlas such as Carington Bowles's *Pocket Atlas of the Counties of South Britain* (1785), or John Cary's *Traveller's Companion*, first issued in 1790, which contains general maps of North and South Wales. (See Olwen Caradoc Evans, *Maps of Wales and Welsh Cartographers*, 1964.)

Acknowledgements

The editors wish to record their grateful thanks to the following individuals who have in various ways assisted them in editing Joseph Hucks's *Pedestrian Tour*: first and foremost to the Right Honourable Lord Aldenham, for many kindnesses including permission to consult and utilize family letters in the Guildhall Library, London, and to the late Dowager Lady Aldenham for allowing us to reproduce the portrait of Joseph Hucks as our frontispiece; to the Master and Mr. R. L. Gooderson of St. Catharine's College, Cambridge; to the Secretary and to Dr. E. S. Leedham-Green, Assistant to the Keeper of the Archives, the University of Cambridge Library; to Mr. Patrick Strong, Keeper of the College Library and Collections, Eton College; to the Librarian, the University of Exeter Library, and to Mr. G. P. Stone, Deputy City Librarian, Exeter City Library; to Dr. A. E. F. Hollaender, formerly Keeper of Manuscripts, the Guildhall Library, London; to the Librarian and the Archivist of the Honourable Society of the Inner Temple Library, London; to Lorna Fraser, the Librarian of Victoria University Library, Toronto; to the Reverend A. R. Leigh, Withycombe Raleigh, Exmouth, Devon; to Mr. Robert Williams, Department of Prints, Drawings, and Maps, National Library of Wales; to the Librarian, the Archivist, and Library Staff of the University College of North Wales, Bangor, and to many of our colleagues there who have answered our queries. Joyce Williams and Lesley Savage have typed several drafts of the manuscript with great skill and enthusiasm.

We also express our gratitude to Jacqueline Tydeman for her work in establishing and illustrating in the accompanying sketch-map the route taken by the travellers.

The editors and publishers gratefully acknowledge the financial support given by Lord and Lady Aldenham towards the printing of the colour Frontispiece.

Preface

In the autumn of 1795 a young Cambridge graduate of 23 published for sale in London, Cambridge, Exeter, and Leeds his first book, *A Pedestrian Tour through North Wales, in a Series of Letters*. Enjoying only a limited circulation at the time, this account of a walking tour undertaken with a companion in the summer of 1794 is today unfamiliar to all but a handful of specialists, and is found on the shelves of only a few British libraries outside London, Oxford, and Cambridge.[1]

Difficult as it is to procure a copy of his book, it is even more difficult to obtain reliable information on its author Joseph Hucks; several authorities erroneously give his Christian name as John and the fullest account of his short life is found in a virtually unknown history mainly concerned with an entirely different family.[2] Yet both Hucks and his book deserve to be more widely celebrated: not only are Joseph Hucks's career, opinions, and beliefs of intrinsic interest as being highly characteristic of their period, but his *Tour* also offers us an invaluable and tantalising glimpse of his travelling companion, a Cambridge man of his own age destined to become one of the greatest figures of the Romantic Movement in England. His name was Samuel Taylor Coleridge.

The present edition is the first reprint of Hucks's *Pedestrian Tour* to appear; appropriately, it is reproduced from an original copy in the possession of the Library of the University College of North Wales, where it was formerly bound up with a copy of the second edition of *A Gentleman's Tour Through Monmouthshire and Wales* by H. Penruddock Wyndham, published by T. Evans in 1794. Hucks's book was published by J. Debrett, Piccadilly, and J. Edwards, Pall Mall; it is in duodecimo form, and contains 160 pages, with a further page of errata which have been silently incorporated into the present

1. The London Library has no copy; the John Rylands Library at Manchester and the university libraries of Leeds and Exeter do not possess one. According to the *National Union Catalog*, only seven American libraries have the work on their shelves, and the extensive collection of Coleridgeana at Victoria University, Toronto does not include a copy of the *Tour*.
2. J. A. Gibbs, *The History of Antony and Dorothea Gibbs* . . . etc., London, 1922, issued in a limited edition of 100 copies.

text. Further obvious misprints have been corrected, short s substituted for long s, and catchwords omitted, but in all other respects, Hucks's original text is reproduced as it stands.

The ensuing introduction begins with as full a biography of Hucks as it has been possible to reconstruct, one which certainly provides a far more detailed picture of his life and career than any which has appeared before. There follows a discussion of the significance of the leading ideas and attitudes found expressed in the *Tour*, and the part which Coleridge may have played in formulating or developing them. Hucks emerges as a man of basically orthodox views and principles who nonetheless shared, even if only briefly, some of the more radical notions of his persuasive touring companion through Wales. Thus, in his reactions to the ferment of ideas current in his day, Hucks may serve as a representative young man of his age, inspired by a moderately revolutionary fervour, yet discreet enough not to advocate the abandonment of all civilized principles. His attitudes also reinforce the generally accepted opinion that Romanticism inherited many of its principal concepts from mid-eighteenth-century thought.

Critical apparatus has been confined to annotations of the major points of topographical, literary, and historical interest in the text, to reprinting Coleridge's surviving letters covering the period of his travels, along with Hucks's poem addressed to his former companion, taken from his *Poems* of 1798, and to the provision of an itinerary offering some guidance to the confusing chronology of the tour. A sketch-map indicates the main places of interest visited by the travellers, the place-names being rendered in their modern forms, Hucks's own gazeteer (pp. 72–3) listing the forms employed in his own day.

University College of North Wales,   Alun R. Jones
Bangor, Gwynedd   William Tydeman

Introduction

I. *Biographical Sketch*

Joseph Hucks, the author of *A Pedestrian Tour through North Wales*, was born at Knaresborough, near Harrogate, Yorkshire, in the latter half of March 1772; the exact date of his birth still remains unknown, but he was christened at Knaresborough on 24 March and thus was some six months older than his celebrated contemporary and companion on the tour of North Wales, Samuel Taylor Coleridge. His father William (1717–82), a wine merchant, was the youngest son of a wealthy London brewer and Middlesex magistrate, a previous Joseph Hucks. All William Hucks's uncles were also in the brewing industry, and several generations of the family had been brewers to the Royal Household in the eighteenth century; their genealogical tree included at least two Members of Parliament. The Huckses traced their ascertained pedigree only as far back as another William Hucks, a brewer of St. Giles-in-the-Fields, Bloomsbury, who died in 1691, but they claimed descent from the Hookes, a prominent family in Conwy, North Wales, the most celebrated of whom lies buried below the chancel floor of Conwy Parish Church with the following inscription, recently restored to legibility, above him:

> Here lyeth Ye Body of Nichs Hookes of Conway Gent. Who was Ye 41 Child of his Father Wm. Hookes Esq. by Alice his Wife, and Ye Father of 27 Children, who dyed Ye 20 Day of March 1637.

Joseph Hucks, during his pedestrian tour, visited his prolific ancestor's tomb out of curiosity, and 'took down the inscription with a pencil'.[1]

1. See page 29 below. There are also slabs commemorating Maria and Dorothye Hookes in the chancel of Conwy Church and a stone wall monument to Hugh Hookes in the south transept, but the lettering on the latter is now so faint as to be almost indecipherable. According to Robert Williams, *The History and Antiquities of the Town of Aberconwy . . .*, Denbigh, 1835, p. 105, it read 'Johanes Hookes, Arm hunc tumulum fieri fecit in memoriam celeberrimi viri Hugonis Hookes, Arm. patris sui, qui obiit 27 die Julii, A.D. 1600'. The name occurs several times in Williams's history, and in Norman Tucker, *Conway and its Story*, Denbigh, 1960, *passim*. See also *An Inventory of the Ancient Monuments in Caernarvonshire*, 1956–64, I. 44 and Plate 47, where the date of death given for Hugh Hookes is 1609 and for Nicholas Hookes 1627.

William Hucks of Knaresborough married in 1749 and had thirteen children by his wife Eleanor, many of whom did not survive infancy or youth; Joseph was the sixth son born to the couple, but three had already died prior to his birth, while his elder brother William died aged 28 in July 1782, the same year as William Hucks Senior; of the male line only John Hucks (1769–1836) lived beyond his thirtieth birthday. Of the surviving daughters, Eleanora (1752–1800) married in 1774 Henry Towneley Ward, a London solicitor, and Dorothea (1760–1820) married in October 1784 Antony Gibbs (1756–1815), a West Country merchant and founder of the London business house which still bears his name. It is because of this marriage that our knowledge of Joseph Hucks's activities is as complete as it is, for the Gibbs family assiduously preserved their personal and business papers over a long period, and the kindness of the present head of the family, the Rt. Hon. Lord Aldenham, and of the authorities at the Guildhall Library in London (where the papers are now housed), has enabled a fairly full account of Joseph Hucks's relatively short life to be assembled. Twenty-seven original letters from Hucks are contained among the Gibbs family letters, (Guildhall MS 11021), and expand the passing references to Joseph Hucks given in J. A. Gibbs's massive study of *The History of Antony and Dorothea Gibbs and of their Contemporary Relatives, including the History of the Origin and Early Years of the House of Antony Gibbs and Sons*,[1] published by the St. Catherine Press, London, in 1922.

At the same time relatively little is known of Joseph's early years; in 1782 he entered Eton College as a King's Scholar, while his brother John attended Harrow. Joseph remained at Eton till 1790 but no records of his school career appear to have survived. At their father's death on 3 July 1782, their married sister Eleanora Ward appears to have taken charge of the boys,[2] while the widowed Mrs. Hucks removed from Knaresborough to Exmouth early in 1784. On 3 October of that year Dorothea Hucks married Antony Gibbs, an exporting woollen merchant from Exeter, and they made their home first in the city itself and then just outside it at Exwick House. The first extant letter of Joseph Hucks's to be preserved is addressed to Dorothea from Eton, on 10 November 1786, congratulating his

1. Hereafter referred to as Gibbs, *History*. It should be pointed out that Gibbs's transcripts of family papers are unfortunately not to be relied upon.
2. The Wards' town house was in Soho Square; Ward carried on his practice at 4 Henrietta St., Covent Garden. In 1784 he built a country house, 'The Willows', on the Thames between Bray and Windsor. By 1800 the Wards were living at 3 Henrietta Street.

sister on a safe delivery of her second child Harriott; in it he informs her:

> I go on very well at Eton have just got my remove,[1] and am reading Virgil & Horace, the first of Which I know you admire. . . .[2]

which indicates that Dorothea Gibbs was herself a woman of some education and taste.

Further evidence for Joseph's activities at Eton is provided by a second letter to Dorothea Gibbs, now resident with her husband in Madrid, dated 10 December 1789, (*FL* III. 295–8) in the course of which he observes:

> . . . The time has run away rather quick with me at Eton, For I practice a good deal on the flute, & I think I like it more and more every day; I have been engag'd in acting plays, which run away with some of my time, I like it very much. I have already play'd in Sheridan's, Rivals, the Midnight hour,[3] & ye beaux Stratagem, & my Mother has been good enough to send me some *Theatricals*. . . .[4] My Dear Sister I leave Eton next August to enter much ye same sort of life at Colledge with the difference only, that more depends upon yr self— . . .

(This letter is endorsed in another hand, presumably that of Mrs. William Hucks; she speaks of Joseph having visited Dulwich, Chatham, and Bath over the Christmas holidays, and informs Dorothea that he returns to Eton on 13 January 1790.)

It was shortly before he left Eton that what appears to be the only existing portrait of Hucks was painted; it is a small full-length portrait by Richard Livesay[5] showing him dressed to take part in the traditional 'Montem' procession, a ceremony for which scholars would don decorative or semi-military costume and set out to Salt

---

1. Promotion to a higher class in the school.
2. *Family Letters*, Collected and Arranged by Henry Hucks Gibbs, 1876, now Guildhall MS 11021, II. 437–9. (This collection is hereafter referred to as *FL*.)
3. A farce, adapted from the French by Elizabeth Inchbald, first performed at Covent Garden in May 1787.
4. Stage properties (costumes?). O.E.D. gives a quotation of 1855 as its earliest example of this meaning.
5. Richard Livesay (c. 1750–1823) was pupil and assistant to Benjamin West; he settled in Windsor c. 1790, and taught drawing to the family of George III. He later became drawing master at the Royal Naval College, Portsmouth. According to the *Dictionary of National Biography*, 'While at Windsor he was much employed painting portraits of young Etonians, generally small whole-lengths, and an interesting picture by him of "Eton Boys going to Montem" is in the possession of the college, to which it was presented by the Duke of Newcastle in 1891.' See also note 1 on p. xii. Hucks must have been one of the first Etonians to be painted by Livesay.

Hill, Slough, where they would elicit contributions from bystanders and passers-by to support the senior colleger at King's College, Cambridge, a custom which continued until 1847.[1] The picture, which shows Hucks dressed for the ceremony on 25 May 1790, seems to have been taken from a larger unfinished canvas formerly hanging in College Hall and now in the new Brewhouse Gallery at Eton, known as 'Eton Boys going to Montem'. Until recently the portrait was in the possession of the late Dowager Lady Aldenham, and she generously gave us permission to photograph the work for reproduction as our frontispiece. In the ceremony on 29 May 1787 Hucks seems to have attended on the Ensign 'Scott', but there is a certain doubt about what office Hucks filled in the 1790 'Montem': in addition to the Captain, Lieutenant, Ensign, Marshall and Sergeant, there were two Salt-bearers with attendant Servitors who, says J. L. Nevinson, were 'posted to collect money as far afield as Maidenhead Bridge, Datchet and Colnbrook'.[2] Gibbs in his *History* (p. 438) states that Hucks acted as a Salt-bearer, but the *Montem Lists 1773–1832* (Eton, 1835) assign this office to 'Hart' and 'Mr. Montague', giving to Hucks the rank of Servitor. This would be consistent with Mrs. Hucks's remark below that her son was 'one of the principal Runners'; besides which the figure in the portrait does not carry the usual bag of salt. However, the lists almost certainly contain inaccuracies. A letter from Mrs. William Hucks to Dorothea Gibbs, dated 1 August 1790, (*FL* III. 402–3) gives a pen-picture of her son's costume just as it appears in the Livesay portrait:

> . . . Joseph has this year or two cost a great deal above a £100 a year, his bill from Eton Since April £45 for Montem as he had a dress on purpose added near £10 to the bill, but I do not grudge it, he is much improved, & they say is likely to be a Handsome Young Man he was one of the principal Runners, & must have look'd well in his dress which was white dimmity with rose Coulourd bows, & large [?] sash to his Breeches & ½ boots the same coulour, an Alexanders Cap with Feathers & as he is pretty Tall it quite became him. . . .

Of the transition from Eton to Cambridge few records have come to light: on 27 May 1790 (two days after the Montem ceremony) Hucks was admitted to St. Catharine's College as a Pensioner (a fee-paying

---

1. For details of the Montem processions see Henry Maxwell-Lyte, *History of Eton College*, 1875, Chapter 21, and J. L. Nevinson, 'Eton College and the origins of the Montem costume', *The Connoisseur*, (October 1972), pp. 88–93, where Livesay's large picture is mentioned. It is reproduced in colour in *Treasures of Eton*, ed. James McConnell, 1976, opp. p.12; Joseph Hucks stands in the foreground on the right.
2. *Op. cit.*, p.89.

student), and in November entered the college of which he remained a member until his death ten years later. His matriculation was recorded on 17 December 1790.[1] Financially this change placed his mother in some difficulty; as she confided to Dorothea Gibbs in a letter of 7 November 1790 (*FL* III. 425–6):

> . . . being such a distance from Cambridge will be attended with a very great expence as it will cost not less than 20 [10?] guineas your Brothers going & coming, which with my other disbursements is incompatible with my income, which from divers causes is very much lessened. The furnishing my House/the poorly/Johns great extravagance fitting Joseph out & furnishing his rooms have been such great drawbacks; as has much reduced me; besides as there are three vacations in the Year was I nearer him, he might come to me [.] now except the long one which is in Summer, he will be obliged to beat up his friends quarters, a circumstance not very agreable, as people may be glad to see you now & then, but it may not be always convenient. . . .

What actually happened is not clear; certainly Hucks never seems to have been a very affluent man. His elder brother John appears to have been notoriously spendthrift: by 1790 he was farming in Ireland, and his subsequent financial affairs and eventual bankruptcy were to cause his lawyer brother great anxiety and much enforced activity on his behalf.

Joseph's commencement in the legal profession was made while he was still an undergraduate: on 5 November 1792 he was admitted as a student of the Inner Temple; in a letter begun on 20 January 1793 (*FL* IV. 163–6), writing from Cambridge to Dorothea Gibbs, after some disparaging remarks on the East Anglian winter scene, Hucks informs her that he has embarked on a legal career:

> . . . Nothing can be duller than this place in Winter; for ye only beauty it at any Time derives is from the thick Foliage of the Trees about it which prevents ye view of the surrounding Country, & consequently when not a leaf, nor a rising Ground are to be seen, & nothing but Fens & Ditches for Miles, the Situation can not be very alluring. Nor must you expect me to entertain you with the News of the place, for being so much out of the World, it of course has none, unless it be a dissertation on ye Walls of My College or the beauty of the Bricks, this I am certainly entitled to do, for the Setting Sun alone Shrouds them from my View, and I will not say the rising Sun, but about Seven in the Morning again presents them to my Eyes. As you have never been in Cambridge Shire you cannot form a proper Idea of the appearance of ye Country; To the only rising Ground they have

1. Information provided by Dr. E. S. Leedham-Green, Assistant to the Keeper of the Archives, University of Cambridge Library.

they give the Magnificent Appellation of the Gogmagog Hills whose perpendicular height from ye summit to the Base I take to be around seven Yards & three Quarters.

I am going to Town next Wednesday to keep my Term in the Temple, Shall Stay about a Week, but Shall not have much of that Time to myself, since it is necessary for me to dine in Hall four Days. They are in great agitation in London concerning the Death of Louis the 16th, whose fate must be lamented by all Europe, exclusive of his inhuman Butchers.[1] . . .

On 31 January 1793 at the Inner Temple Hucks entered into the customary £50 bond against his charges for Commons and other membership dues, Henry Towneley Ward standing as one of his sureties. Hucks is recorded as having lived in Commons during two weeks of each of the terms between Hilary Term 1793 and Easter Term 1798, by which time he had fulfilled the current requirements for being called to the bar. However, he was never called, since in his chosen sphere as a Special Pleader it was not necessary for him to be called in order to practise. However, Hucks may have planned to be called in due course, had death not prevented him.[2]

On 3 April 1794 Hucks graduated as a Bachelor of Arts of the University, being placed third among the Junior Optimes,[3] and shortly after graduating he became involved in a college dispute concerning the election of a Skerne Fellow on the Ramsden foundation. W. H. S. Jones, in his history of St. Catharine's College, says that a vacancy occurred in March 1794 and on the day of election, 22 April, there were three candidates: Hucks, Richard Foster, and Richard Wadsworth. Of the seven electors six voted for Foster and one for Wadsworth, so that Foster was declared elected as Skerne Fellow. However, Wadsworth appealed to the Lord Chancellor to set Foster's election aside on the ground of his being 'superannuated', and to declare himself duly elected. It was not until 14 March 1795 that the Master and Fellows presented a petition to the Lord Chancellor, praying him to hear Wadsworth's appeal against the election of Richard Foster as Skerne Fellow and the result was that an order was served on all the parties concerned to attend the hearing of the appeal in the Court of Chancery on 23 March 1795; eventually Foster was debarred, though he received stipend up to Lady Day 1795. On 6 April 1795 Joseph Hucks was duly admitted Fellow on

1. Louis XVI of France was executed on 21 January 1793, which suggests that Hucks's letter was composed over a period of some days.
2. We owe this information to the Librarian of the Inner Temple and his staff.
3. *The Names in the Cambridge Triposes, from 1754 to 1807*, Bath, 1808, p.28. Junior Optimes were those placed in the third division of the Mathematical Tripos.

the Ramsden foundation and, as Jones wrily observes, 'one can only guess why Wadsworth was ignored.'[1]

It was in the summer vacation of 1794 that Hucks toured North Wales with Coleridge, and subsequently wrote the account of it which is reprinted for the first time in these pages. How well acquainted the travelling companions were prior to their journey together is uncertain: they were not members of the same college, for Coleridge was from Jesus College, which he entered in October 1791, and there seems to be no way of knowing how the two men met, or what degree of friendship existed between them at Cambridge. There is no reference to their travels in Hucks's existing writings, outside the *Tour* itself and a few poems, and Coleridge's letters provide no information as to what plans, or advance preparations the pair made, if any. Coleridge's first extant reference to Hucks is scarcely complimentary: it comes in a celebrated anecdote contained in a letter to Robert Southey, addressed from Gloucester on Sunday 6 July 1794:

> . . . It is *wrong*, Southey! for a little Girl with a half-famished sickly Baby in her arms to put her head in at the window of an Inn—'Pray give me a bit of Bread and Meat'! from a Party dining on Lamb, Green Pease, & Sallad—Why?? Because it is *impertinent* & *obtrusive*!— I am a Gentleman!—and wherefore should the clamorous Voice of Woe *intrude* upon mine Ear!?'
>
> My companion is a Man of cultivated, tho' not vigorous, understanding—his feelings are all on the side of humanity—yet such are the unfeeling Remarks, which the lingering Remains of Aristocracy occasionally prompt. . . .[2]

The travellers appear to have left Cambridge about 15 June, and then spent three weeks in Oxford, where Coleridge met for the first time Robert Southey; Hucks made the poet's acquaintance too, and Coleridge sends Southey Hucks's compliments in both letters written on the tour. On Saturday 5 July the tour finally began, and took the friends into Wales by way of Gloucester, Ross-on-Wye, Hereford, Leominster, and Bishop's Castle (see sketch-map). That the travellers discussed many matters together *en route* goes without saying, even were the evidence provided by the *Tour* lacking; Hucks told his companion of a friend who

1. W. H. S. Jones, *A History of St. Catharine's College, once Catharine Hall, Cambridge*, Cambridge, 1936, p. 125. We owe this reference to Mr. R. N. Gooderson, Fellow of St. Catharine's College, Cambridge.
2. See *The Collected Letters of S. T. Coleridge*, ed. E. L. Griggs, Oxford, 1956–71, (referred to hereafter as *Letters*), I. 83–4 (Coleridge's letters describing the tour appear in Appendix, I, pages 91–104 below).

> . . . after long struggles between Principle and *Interest* (as it is
> improperly called) accepted a place under Government—he took the
> Oaths—shuddered—went home and threw himself in an Agony out of
> a two pair of stairs' Window![1]

and Coleridge admits that on much of the route one of his pastimes
was 'philosophizing with Hucks'. Indeed Southey may have felt that
there was an intimacy between his new-found friend and his
Cambridge companion from which he, the Oxonian, was excluded,
and probably observed as much to Coleridge, for the latter replies in
his letter from Wrexham:

> Warmth of particular Friendship does not imply absorption. The
> nearer you approach the Sun, the more intense are his Rays—yet what
> distant corner of the System do they not cheer and vivify? The ardour
> of private Attachments makes Philanthropy a necessary *habit* of the
> Soul. I love my *Friend*—such as *he* is, all mankind are or *might be*! The
> deduction is evident. . . .
>
> What did you mean by *H.* has '*my understanding*'? I have puzzled
> myself in vain to discover the import of the sentence. The only sense it
> *seemed* to bear was so like *mock-humility*, that I scolded myself for the
> momentary supposition.—. . . .[2]

It is of course possible that the reference to 'H' alludes to someone
other than Hucks, but it would be reasonable to assume that for the
period of the tour at least Coleridge and Hucks were on terms of
close friendship, though it is impossible to say whether the relationship remained a warm one after the tour, since all sources of
information are silent on the point.

It has even been suggested by Professor Kathleen Coburn that
Hucks was to have been one of the Pantisocrats whom Coleridge and
Southey proposed to lead in the establishment of a Utopian community on the banks of the Susquehanna river in Pennsylvania.[3]
When, in March 1836, Southey came to reminisce about the scheme
to Joseph Cottle, his words certainly suggested that Hucks was
present at the preliminary Oxford discussions from which Pantisocracy sprang:

> In the summer of 1794, S.T.C. and Hucks came to Oxford on their
> way into Wales for a pedestrian tour. There Allan [*sic*] introduced
> them to me, and the scheme was talked of, but by no means

1. *Letters*, I. 85.
2. *Letters*, I. 86.
3. *The Notebooks of S. T. Coleridge*, ed. K. Coburn, 1956 (hereafter referred to as
   Notebooks), I. 161 note. For the background see also J. R. MacGillivray, 'The
   Pantisocratic Scheme and its Immediate Background', in M. W. Wallace (ed),
   Studies in English . . ., Toronto, 1931, pp.130–69.

determined on. It was talked into shape by Burnett and myself, when upon the commencement of the Long Vacation, we separated from them, they making for Gloucester, he and I proceeding on foot to Bath. . . . .[1]

But Professor Coburn's claim that Hucks was himself actually of the Pantisocratic brethren is unsupported by any of the lists of provisional settlers so far discovered. J. R. MacGillivray is possibly partly responsible for this misleading impression since he writes 'on Sunday, August 3rd, after trudging six hundred miles up hill and down dale, preaching pantisocracy and aspheterism to all comers, Coleridge and Hucks arrived in Bristol to rejoin their fellow-citizens of the new Commonwealth' (*op. cit*, p. 159). Of course, it is not implausible that Coleridge's youthful enthusiasm, expressed frequently and at length during the tour, made one further but only temporary convert to the doctrines of Pantisocracy. As Coleridge tells Southey in the letter begun on 13 July, 'I have positively done nothing but dream of the System of no Property every step of the Way since I left you',[2] and he doubtless expatiated persuasively on his dreams to his companion. Certainly, on his return to Cambridge, he wrote to Southey on 18 September 1794 that Brooke and Berdmore, whom Hucks and Coleridge encountered in North Wales (see p. 29 below), 'have spread my Opinions in mangled forms at Cambridge',[3] which suggests that *they* had learnt of pantisocracy from Coleridge while in Wales, but there is no evidence that Joseph Hucks ever planned to make the journey to the banks of the Susquehanna.

One further curious link between the travelling companions may be noted, namely a common interest in the Latin lyrics of the Polish poet Casimir (Sarbiewski Maciej Kazimierz [1595–1640]). In December 1793 when Coleridge fled from Cambridge to join the Light Dragoons, he sold three books to a Reading bookseller including 'a very valuable Edition of Casimir by Balbou,' (that published in Paris in 1759), which he was able to redeem upon his discharge from the army in March 1794, but which he had lost again by 1 September when he informed Southey in a letter: 'I lost my Casimir on the Road'.[4] His plan was to make a series of translations from modern Latin poets including Casimir, and the prospectus for

1. *New Letters of Robert Southey*, ed. Kenneth Curry, New York, 1965, II. 446 (hereafter referred to as *New Letters*). For Allen and Burnett, see note 1, p. 93 and note 1, p. 94.
2. *Op cit.*, I. 90.
3. *Ibid*, I. 103.
4. *Ibid*, I. 97.

the proposed volume (*Proposals for publishing by Subscription Imitations from the Modern Latin Poets*) appeared as an advertisement dated 10 June and signed 'S.T.C.' in the *Cambridge Intelligencer* for 14 June and 26 July 1794, promising among other features 'a copious Selection from the Lyrics of Casimir'. Coleridge may well have brought copies of the text of his advertisement with him to Oxford, as Southey mentions the *Imitations* in a letter completed on 19 June.[1] The two volumes 'by S. T. Coleridge, of Jesus College, Cambridge' are advertised to be 'ready for delivery shortly after the next Christmas'.

But although Coleridge told his brother George in a letter of 26 March that he had 'finished two or three Odes of Casimir',[2] only one translation seems to have survived (to be found in the *Poetical Works*, ed. E. H. Coleridge, 1912, I. 59). Professor Coburn suggests (*Notebooks* I. 161 Note) that it was Isaac Watts (1674–1748) whose imitations of Casimir inspired Coleridge to emulate his example; certainly Coleridge refers to them approvingly in *The Watchman* for 9 March 1796 where his own version of Casimir's 'Ad Lyram' Book II Ode 3 first appeared. He also quotes from the Polish writer in *Biographia Literaria* (the fifth ode of the third Book) and goes on to praise Casimir's style and diction as truly classical, 'while Cowley, who resembles Casimir in many respects, compleatly barbarizes *his* Latinity, and even his metre, by the heterogeneous nature of his thoughts'.[3]

It is clear therefore that in the summer of 1794 the poetry of Casimir was a subject very much on Coleridge's mind, and it is probably of significance that Hucks's *Poems* of 1798 also contains translations from Casimir's works, one by Hucks himself ('To a Stream' from Casimir's Epigram 21, *Poems*, p. 92) and several by his friend, William Heald[4]—one being Casimir's Ode 3 from Book II (*Poems*, p. 181), the same 'Ad Lyram' translated by Coleridge.[5] Indeed, it may be conjectured whether it was not Coleridge who introduced Hucks to Casimir's work on the North Wales tour, whether indeed the 'very valuable Edition' accompanied them on their way, and whether the notion of a possible collaboration on the projected volume of *Imitations* was proposed; certainly we may infer that Coleridge might have welcomed Hucks's assistance, since by 21

1. *Ibid*, I. 82, note 1.
2. *Ibid*, I. 77.
3. Ed. J. Shawcross, Oxford, 1907, II. 209.
4. See p. xxv below.
5. The others were 'To the Grasshopper' (Book IV. Ode 23) and 'To the Rose' (Book IV. Ode 18) (*Poems*, pp.183–4).

October 1794 the poet was admitting to Southey that 'My Imitations too depress my spirits—the task is arduous and grows upon me.'[1] These suggestions must remain speculative, but it is surely more than coincidental that Hucks and Coleridge both made translations from the same modern Latin author, and that they should have been in close contact when the projected *Imitations* was in the forefront of Coleridge's thoughts.

The tour seems to have ended early in August; on 5 August Coleridge was writing to Robert Lovell from Bristol enquiring as to Southey's whereabouts,[2] and according to J. A. Gibbs (*History*, p. 94) Mrs. Hucks's diary records the return of her son thus on 4 August:

Joseph arrived from his tour through Wales, walked 700 miles. . . .[3]

Henry Hucks Gibbs, who arranged the collection of family papers in 1876, alludes to a family tradition when he records that 'it was overwalking himself on this Tour which sowed the seeds of the Consumption of which he died',[4] but there would appear to be no necessary connection between the two facts. However, on several occasions in the *Pedestrian Tour* Hucks mentions colds and a sore throat, which may have some significance in tracing the growth of his infirmity.[5]

By the end of August Joseph is heard of again, accompanying his brother-in-law Antony Gibbs to Falmouth to see him embark for a further period of business activity in Spain; a bad carriage accident in February 1793 had forced Gibbs to spend a year recuperating in England, and he was now anxious to recultivate his Spanish connections. Hucks returned to Exeter by sea, and in due course resumed his studies at Cambridge. A letter of 22 January 1795 (*FL* IV. 335–6), addressed to Dorothea, contains a cheerful self-portrait of the budding lawyer:

. . . I stick hard to the Desk—The first opportunity I have, I will send you my Portrait with the Quill behind my Ear. A future wig hung up on the Peg behind me & the whole body of Reports, Statutes at large etc suspended from the Ceiling by a single thread . . .

A Pedestrian Tour through North Wales, in a Series of Letters by J. Hucks, B.A., appeared in 1795, published by two London booksel-

1. *Op. cit.*, I. 116.
2. *Ibid*, I. 96.
3. The table at the end of the tour records the distance walked as far as Bristol as 629 miles.
4. *FL* V. 99.
5. See pages 35, 43, 47 below.

lers, J. Debrett of Piccadilly, and J. Edwards of Pall Mall. It was also sold by three Cambridge booksellers, Lunn, Flower and Deighton, by Messrs. Binns and Greenwood of Leeds, and by Messrs. Dyer and Trewman, of Exeter.[1] It was a small duodecimo volume of some 160 pages and unlike many travel-books of the time, without illustrations; there is no way of ascertaining the number of copies printed, but it is unlikely to have been large, the work presumably being published at the author's expense. Hucks was later to regret that he had been quite so generous with presentation copies of the *Tour*; he observed in a letter to Dorothea of 4 August 1797 (*FL* V. 57–60), when offering her a copy of his forthcoming *Poems*:

> I shall be shy of *giving* this time; for I gave away all my profits the last; and was out of pocket besides; & tho I do not scribble to gain, yet I am far from wishing to lose . . .

Although its present whereabouts cannot be traced, it is fairly certain that a copy of the *Tour* would have made its way, as from one travelling companion to another, to Coleridge now living at Nether Stowey; certainly he received a presentation copy of Hucks's *Poems* in 1798, for it is now housed in the Library of Victoria College, University of Toronto, whose Librarian has generously made it available on microfilm to the present editors.

The years 1795 and 1796 appear to have been fairly uneventful ones for Hucks: in April 1795 he was elected a Fellow of his Cambridge college in circumstances already described.[2] He doubtless studied hard and enjoyed the congenial life of a Cambridge common-room and the Inner Temple, while remaining a conscientious and devoted member of both the Hucks and Gibbs family circles. On 19 April 1796 Antony Gibbs's sister Anne (1757–1828) married Samuel Banfill, an Exeter businessman, and Gibbs's one-time partner; on hearing of the engagement, Joseph informed Dorothea on 16 February 1796 (*FL* IV. 407–9):

> . . . I sincerely think with you—that He will be happy with her and also that He fully deserves to be so—He has faults so has every body—perhaps his are more conspicuous therefore less blame-

1. In 1798 Flower (a printer), Deighton and Lunn, and J. Debrett of Piccadilly were involved in the publication of Hucks's *Poems*; others named are J. Nicholson, G. G. and J. Robinson of Paternoster Row, and T. Conder of Bucklersbury, London. Lunn and Flower were involved in the publication of Coleridge's *Fall of Robespierre* in 1794, G. G. and J. Robinson published his *Poems on Various Subjects* in 1796.
2. See pp. xiv–xv above.

able—Upon the whole I believe He has an excellent heart, is a sincere friend, and a man of much discernment & more than common abilities, tho in a particular line. . . .[1]

In the early summer of 1796 Mrs. Hucks, Joseph, Dorothea and the Gibbs children all removed to a new house near Exwick, half a mile north-west of Exeter; called Lower Cleave, it was rented from Thomas Northmore who lived nearby at Cleave House. Northmore (1766–1851), a former pupil of Coleridge's father, had edited a work by Tryphiodorus in 1791 and Plutarch's *Treatise Upon the Distinction between a Friend and a Flatterer, with Remarks* in 1795. In 1799 his edition of Gray's *Tour through England and Wales* appeared.[2] In a letter of 23 June 1796 (*FL* IV. 449–51), written to Antony engaged on business in Edinburgh, Hucks told him of the new home, and particularly its garden:

> As to *Lower Cleve*, which you have heard of, I am confirmed in my opinion that it is a very pretty spot, & such a one as you might look out for, a long time, without success—. The Garden, which when we first came was a 'wild where weeds & flowers promiscuous grew'[3] has now lost the unseemliness of its beauty, & got on its gayest apparel—The walk is weedless,—the Woodbine & the dark Ivy cling around the larger Trees, nor does the unodoriferous Hemlock or Touch-forbidding thistle any longer offend their pride—The Stubborn Clods of the Garden bow beneath the sturdy stroke of the Spade & Maddock [sic], & the apples of the Earth will soon rear their taste-inviting heads. The South West umbragenous fence smiles & flourishes after the labours of my rake & sickle—The waving horors of the lawn have humbled themselves to the Earth before the all destroying Scythe, & are converted into wholesome nourishment for the most useful & the most noble of all Quadrupeds—

In the following March Antony was able to inspect the new property for himself, since political events in Spain forced him to return to England for nearly two years of enforced inactivity.

1797 also saw Joseph Hucks crossed in love, the only romantic attachment of which the extant letters provide evidence. The object of his affections was Louisa Oakden, a protegée of his married sister, Eleanora Ward, described by John Hucks's wife Matilda as 'a most

1. Banfill was a textile manufacturer with a factory at Exwick; after Antony Gibbs's business failure of 1789, Banfill seems to have taken over Exwick House, residing there till 1830. He was generous-hearted, but renowned for his conceit, affectation and obstinacy. (Gibbs, *History*, pp.21, 58, 101.)
2. *Notebooks*, I. 505 Note.
3. Cf. Pope, *An Essay on Man*, Epistle I. 7: 'A wild, where weeds and flow'rs promiscuous shoot'.

elegant young woman and as good as pleasing',[1] but his rival was a French businessman, Jacques Courant, who succeeded in winning Louisa's hand after nearly five years' courtship. One would surmise that Hucks became attracted to Louisa somewhat later than did Courant, and, it appears, won her regard, but his lack of means may have been the chief obstacle to their engagement, and Courant, despite the failure of his Cadiz business house in 1796, married Louisa on 12 March 1797. This marriage, which the Wards felt to be hasty and ill-advised, caused tension and an eventual breach between Louisa and Eleanora Ward, which remained unrepaired up to the latter's death in 1800. Joseph Hucks evidently made *his* disappointment all too manifest, and it was no doubt in response to his brother-in-law's admonishments that he wrote to Antony Gibbs on 13 May 1797 (*FL* V. 23–6):

> I received yr kind letter & having according to your desire, read it over many times & considered its contents with that attention which it deserved, I shall now trouble you with my reply to it. And in the first place be assured that I have undergone such a change as to be perfectly ashamed of the weakness I have exhibited. My resolution that has played the truant so long is returned—Not but what I shall *ever* consider it as a misfortune, & a very great one; of which neither the lapse of time nor change of place can alter the complexion: Philosophy does not consist of a *want* of passions or of feeling, but rather in the perpetual endeavour to overcome them; & in that happy art which is only known to a few of extracting good out of evil, & of rendering the misfortunes of life an ultimate advantage to the mind. But me! Do not my Dear Friend insult me with the name of a Philosopher; I who in this instance have violated its plainest principles, its most evident Axioms. She was free to act as She did, & I had no right to reflect upon her conduct, & if what She did, has produced her happiness, I ought to be, as indeed I now am, sincerely rejoiced. And yet by the most idle & effeminate complaints I have hitherto proved myself incapable either to rejoice at or to submit to this decision of fate . . . I agree with you, it would be wrong *at present* to cultivate a *close intimacy* there, but it will be impossible for me to absent myself entirely. I must banish myself not only from *her*, but from all our common friends where I may have a chance of meeting her; Soho Square I shall certainly see as seldom as I do Cleve—If I meet Courant in the street I must run away like a thief who is conscious He has stolen or wishes to steal his most valuable possession. And as I have once been there, what will Courant think of my conduct? He will certainly say 'This man is still in *loaf* with my *Vife*' & therefore I shall be an object of jealousy and suspicion to him. At present this is not the case; For I did not mention it to him in the

1. Gibbs, *History*, p.114.

manner you seem to think I did. What I said upon that head was in a laughing sort of way, & what any one might have done without the least degree of imprudence. Besides I know He thought nothing of it; as soon as I was gone He went up to his *Vife* whom he so much *loafs*, told her what had passed, & congratulated her upon having acquired a Brother in her former friend. Upon the whole; the Question is this: Am I to refrain from going there, & lay myself under the most serious inconveniences for years, certainly as long as we three inhabit the Earth together;? Or shall I endeavour totally to overcome this foolish regret for the past; & go & be received there as a Friend without suspicion?

However, by May 1798 Courant's financial affairs were in a desperate state, and he and his wife left England for Hamburg; they eventually settled in Poissy, north-west of Paris, from whence Louisa wrote an effusively concerned letter to Dorothea Gibbs in July 1800 (*FL* V. 683–5) when she learnt of Joseph's fatal illness. The tone of this letter and the fact that she gave her mare into his keeping on her departure from England, suggest that she still regarded her English suitor with affection, if not with love. Joseph himself (though not, of course, an unbiassed witness) regarded her future with grave misgivings: writing to Dorothea on 20 May 1798 (*FL* V. 135–8) to inform her of the departure for Hamburg, he observed:

> Poor Louisa, She I fear is not wedded to perfect happiness, may all the blessings of heaven go with her: I don't know my Dear Sister how it is, but I feel that my happiness is implicated in hers, I think I have overcome that *kind* of attachment which I once had for her, I think Reason has shown me my weakness, & given me some resolution; time has had its usual effects but Good God what a time![1]

Yet in other respects Hucks was a fairly contented man in 1797; as early as 25 April (*FL* V. 19–20) he told Antony that he intended to pass the whole of the Long Vacation in study:

> . . . My intention is to live in the utmost retirement at Cambridge; indeed I shall have no other choise for I shall have the whole Coll. to myself after the 12 or 15 July. I shall not want employment for I have a great deal to do in the way of reading & writing. I shall live the life of a Hermit. . . .

In the course of his letter of 13 May (*FL* V. 23–6) he tells him again:

> . . . I *cannot* leave London till the 20 June, & I must be at Cam: on the 30. If I do not take my Degree I lose my Fellowship: & tho the

1. Courant died in 1814, leaving Louisa to bring up a family of seven children (Gibbs, *History*, p.116).

Commencement[1] is not till the 4th July, yet we must be there the Saturday before. . . .

Having duly taken his M.A. degree on 4 July, Hucks settled down to spend the summer in legal study but, as he admitted to Dorothea on 4 August (*FL* V. 57–60), his leisure time was also occupied:

> . . . The truth is I am most sedulously employed in the cultivation of the muses; and as I do not chuse to diminish the portion of time allotted to the flowery fictions of the law, I am under the necessity of working double tides; & between you & I, this was the fundamental reason why I determined upon Cambridge for my summer's residence; well knowing that had I staid in Devon: surrounded by so many powerful attractions for the eye and for the heart. the muse & myself might have stood supplicating each other to eternity; or in other words we should have made eternal love without being ever united in the holy bands of matrimony: The beloved offspring of my imagination will be in the press in a short time: & a copy will reach you in about six weeks or two months: I shall be shy of *giving* this time; for I gave away all my profits the last; & was out of pocket besides; & tho I do not scribble to gain, yet I am far from wishing to lose.
>
> You may propagate this my intention of publishing a volume of poems, amongst our friends; that they who choose may buy. . . .

The volume, entitled simply *Poems*, by J. Hucks, A.M. Fellow of Catharine Hall, Cambridge, must have been published early in 1798, for on 21 February, Dorothea was told in a letter (*FL* V. 111–14):

> If the Vol: of poems has afforded you the least degree of amusement, it will be a circumstance highly flattering to my vanity; but I do not reckon much upon the Opinions of my Friends and acquaintance with respect to their merit, because I am well aware, that they are in general dictated by politeness & friendship. I sent 24 Copies to Trewman [the Exeter bookseller], & I hereby give & demise the profits thereof issuing, to Henry[2] to be laid out in the purchase of a Hat or of books or any thing else: tho by the bye I don't believe I have ever given Harriott[3] anything; therefore I leave to your discretion either to buy her a thread case with Scissars etc. with the whole; or to divide it between them as you may think proper: I must however premise, that the Sum will not purchase much; for upon a Supposition Trewman sells them all, his charge upon Commission will reduce it to £3 or thereabouts[4] . . .

---

1. The Cambridge degree ceremony.
2. Dorothea and Antony Gibbs's eldest son, George Henry (1785–1842).
3. The Gibbs's eldest daughter, Harriott (1786–1865).
4. The volume, according to the title-page, cost 3/6. Trewman presumably charged commission of 1/- on every copy.

The volume itself contained thirty-three of Hucks's poems, including ten sonnets, a lengthy reflective piece entitled *The Retrospect*, written in Thomsonian blank-verse and occasioned by Hucks's hatred of military conflict in Europe, and the 'Lines addressed to S. T. Coleridge',[1] in which the author calls his distinguished contemporary 'my earliest friend', and speaks of

> those fair days
> That saw us musing on the willowy banks
> Of Granta's lazy stream; or journeying on,
> Elate with youthful hope, o'er Cambrian wilds;
> Toiling with weary feet, up the steep hill
> Precipitous, o'er many a huge rough rock,
> Or thro' the lengthening vale, or deep-worn glen,
> Dark with impending woods; aye big with schemes
> Air-built, of never fading happiness:[2]
> Wild dreams of folly in the vacant hour,
> That I once fondly cherish'd . . .   (lines 23–33)

In the preface Hucks deprecates his talent for writing verses but excuses them:

> They are the first essays of the author in the field of poetry: they will in all probability also be his last. Far other pursuits in life totally preclude the cultivation of so pleasing an art. . . . The little merit these poems may possess, they owe to the retirement in which they were written; in quitting this, the Author is obliged also to relinquish his favourite pursuit . . .   (pp. iii–iv)

As if further to defend his own muse, Hucks appended to the collection two elegies and five translations by a friend, William Heald (1767–1837), a fellow-Yorkshireman from Dewsbury Moor and a fellow-pensioner of Catharine Hall, who also graduated B.A. in 1794, proceeding M.A. in 1798. Heald had first trained and practised as a surgeon and apothecary at Wakefield, but after graduating, took Holy Orders, becoming Curate of Bobsham, near Cambridge, then Curate of Birstal, near Leeds, in which parish he remained as Vicar from 1801 till June 1836. While a medical student in Edinburgh, he published a mock-heroic poem *The Brunoniad*, and in 1794 his *Farewell Ode on a Distant Prospect of Cambridge* was published in Cambridge. *Moscow: An Ode* followed in 1813.[3]

Several of Hucks's poems seem to have been inspired by public themes: *The Retrospect* reflects on warfare and conquest, the fall of

1. Printed as Appendix II, pages 105–7 below.
2. Another possible indication that Coleridge talked Pantisocracy on the tour and Hucks contributed ideas to the scheme. See pp. xvi–xvii above.
3. For Heald, see *D.N.B.*, and *Alumni Cantabrigiensis*.

empire and the conscience of the individual, while *The Philanthropist* considers the suffering of the poor and schemes for its alleviation, by referring particularly to the work of John Howard, the prison reformer who died on 20 January 1790. Others (chiefly Odes and Invocations) are dedicated to Pity, Truth, Liberty, Nature and Hope in typical eighteenth-century apostrophic vein, while occasional poems such as 'On leaving Cambridge', 'On cutting down a favourite Coppice', 'To the river Thames' are conventionally-worded expressions of commonplace feelings. The lines on the ruins of Denbigh Castle which first appeared, of course, in the *Pedestrian Tour* were now printed in an expanded version[1] and the sonnet '*Written After a Tour*' was probably composed following the visit to North Wales in 1794.

Hucks's vacation labours in Cambridge were partly forced upon him by financial necessity; on 14 November 1797 (*FL* V. 83–6) he confesses to Dorothea that he has, in fact, enjoyed a brief respite from his studies during a three-week holiday in Yorkshire, but goes on to admit:

> . . . in truth I never was poorer, and nothing but the most *frigid economy* will prevent me from becoming a burden to my excellent Mother, which I cannot think of with comfort. . . .

He returns to the subject of his poverty in a letter to Antony, dated from London on 17 December (*FL* V. 95–7) and goes on to allude to Pitt's recently proposed increase in taxes, showing himself once again to be an implacable enemy of the war with France:

> . . . I find myself in the common predicament of many millions upon the surface of this earth, (viz) of not being able to do as I could wish, but this is no uncommon case with me, & it is unavailing to complain. . . .
>
> Pitt has got into an awkward scrape with respect to the assessed taxes:[2] I am of opinion he will persevere in carrying it thro the house, under such modifications as will render it absolutely unproductive: it is impossible it can pass as it is; the clamour is unanimous against its present shape: and the Cities of London Westminster & Southwark are unanimous even against the *principle* of it: Should he persist in it: his Majority in this, as in all other instances, will be ready enough to support him: but depend upon it, it will shake his popularity in the

---

1. See pp. 78–9 below.
2. On 24 November 1797 Pitt proposed to treble the assessed taxes which were levied on a variety of domestic and household items including dogs, carriages, servants and time-pieces. See William Hunt and Reginald L. Poole, *The Political History of England*, X (1760–1801), 1905, p.400. We owe this information to Dr. A. D. Dyer, of the University College of North Wales.

Country: What a wretched politician is John Bull, he will submit to see the liberty he has enjoyed, frittered away under the most frivolous & false pretences; He will give his sanction to the slaughter of a million of his fellow creatures, sacrificed in a cause which has never interested *him*, which if successful can benefit him not at all, & cannot be terminated in either case, without misery & mischief to half the globe: but the moment you come to deprive him of any of his Comforts, (tho he ought to have foreseen that it must inevitably happen) he who was the first to support the whole system of prodigality in money & in blood, is now the first to cry out against it: Nay such a good easy animal does Ministry think him; that in their estimation he is to be dazled with a Puppet Show; If there ever was a farce under heaven acted, it will be the intended procession to Saint Pauls. . . .[1]

Mr. Pitt was this morning burnt in effigy by the populace with this inscription 'The Brother of the ferocious & tyrannical Robespierre'. There will be ten thousand troops to protect the puppet shew to morrow.[2] In short the whole Nation is as mad as a March Hare . . .

Hucks spent Christmas 1797 with the Wards at 'The Willows' between Bray and Windsor, where he may have seen something of Mrs. Courant and her husband, and then presumably returned to his chambers in No. 9 Inner Temple Lane[3], which he occupied until January 1800 when he removed to No. 4. He continued to be oppressed by debts; to Dorothea's request that he should spend the summer of 1798 with the family in Devonshire, he replied in his letter of 21 February (*FL* V. 111–14):

I cannot leave London till late this Year, & my destination is I am sorry to say Cambridge; otherwise my first object & wish would be to pass the Summer Vacation with you. . . . I profited so much in the reading way, & something in pecuniary matters last Summer, that I think it will be highly expedient & advantageous, to repeat the

1. A Thanksgiving for the Naval Victories of the First of June 1794, Cape St. Vincent (14 Feb. 1797), and Camperdown (11 Oct. 1797) was held in St. Paul's Cathedral on 19 December 1797. Pitt's unpopularity was reflected by his being hooted and threatened by the London mob (See *ibid.*, p.400).
2. i.e. the 19th. Hucks's letter was evidently resumed and completed on 18 December.
3. The Archivist of the Inner Temple Library has informed us that staircases in Inner Temple have never numbered more than five, and that this 'may be an error', but it occurs on many of Hucks's letters in the Guildhall Library. (See also p. xxxii below). Hucks was never an official tenant of chambers in Inner Temple Lane, but presumably followed the common practice of renting them from the official owner. The Archivist conjectures that possibly Hucks rented chambers in No. 1 Inner Temple Lane, which was at the Fleet Street end of the west side and could have accommodated *nine* sets of chambers (having four floors above ground level); hence his chambers might have been referred to as '9 Inner Temple Lane'.

measure the ensuing Summer; for with all my assiduity I could not during my last residence completely read thro the two hundred thousand Volumes, the Libraries contain. . . .

However, the invitation evidently was repeated more pressingly, for on 20 May Hucks writes to his sister again (*FL* V. 135–8):

I fear my Dear Sister I must mope away this Summer at Cambridge instead of enjoying much happier hours with you all at Cleve. But I am like the rest of the world very poor & absolutely am compelled to the plan: It is no small part of the evil that this cursed money should deprive me of the power of seeing those I love: Alas it has already fatally debarred me of one happiness, which worlds of riches can now never never make me possess! . . . I shall have Louisa's Mare with me at Cambridge, She has left it in my Care,[1] tho' I shall scarce have the heart to ride her. . . .

Antony Gibbs seems to have added his persuasions to those of his wife, for Joseph writes from Cambridge on July 3 to inform his brother-in-law of the situation (*FL* V. 145–8):

. . . In the first place then, I am, like the rest of the world, poor: And for one of my limited income £65 is a very considerable object, & that Sum I shall lose if I leave Cambridge for more than eleven days at a time this Summer: It were useless to say any more, for really this money is so necessary to satisfy the demands of importunate Creditors, that (tho' it is with disgust & mortification I confess it) it is not in my power to be generous enough to abandon it. . . .

In the next place, I have a great deal which I must go thro with, in the way of my profession, to effect which a large law library is a sine quâ non, nay it is so necessary that had there not luckily been a very valuable & extensive collection of law books here, I believe I must (what would have been still worse than all) have staid in London the whole Vacation. In the 3rd place I have been sworn into the office of Proctor which is one of the principle offices of the University & obliges me to be upon the spot, unless it be for a few days absence, for no business which affects the University as a body, can pass without he is present. . . .

I promise my Sister to come down at Xmas or before, & stay a Month. My business is not at an end here, till the beginning of October. . . .

From the records of Cambridge University we may discover that Hucks was sworn in as Deputy Proctor by a grace of 11 June 1798, in the absence of Martin Joseph Naylor of Queen's College, a proctor for 1797–8, and remained in office until October, when the new proctors were elected. While it was not obligatory at that period for

1. The Courants left for Hamburg about mid-May 1798. See p. xxiii above.

the proctors to remain in Cambridge, the time-consuming nature of their duties made it virtually impossible for them to be absent from the University for very long. Hucks presumably agreed to serve, knowing that he intended to be in Cambridge for the whole of the summer. On the same day he was also elected to the Mathematical Lectureship, one of four (the others founded by Sir Robert Rede) commonly known as the 'Barnaby' lectureships: by this date they had fallen into abeyance, and no lectures were expected of the incumbents elected, though a stipend of £4 per annum was paid to those chosen. There is little to suggest that merit played much part in the selection procedure but perhaps impecuniosity was a qualification: Hucks defeated his rival nominee for the lectureship by five votes to two.[1]

There seems to be no record as to whether or not Hucks's promise to spend Christmas 1798 with the Gibbs family and his mother was fulfilled, but he would appear to have been resident chiefly in London from October 1798 until he left it in April 1799 to stay with his brother John Hucks and his wife in Leeds. In June 1799 he paid a visit to the West Country. Finding nobody in residence at Lower Cleave 'except a certain Hand Maiden who is as Ugly as Sin,' he made a short excursion with a friend along the coast as far as Plymouth, and then returned to Lower Cleave the day before Mrs. Hucks arrived home. The letter which provides this information, written from Lower Cleave to Antony Gibbs, now in Lisbon, and dated 24 August—5 September (*FL* V. 427A-30), is the first in which Hucks mentions symptoms of ill-health in himself:

> . . . My Sister is plagued with a very bad cold & cough, & as for me, whether it be out of complaisance or Sympathy, I certainly keep her Company in both those disorders, & that to the utmost stretch of politeness. . . .

Evidently the highlight of the stay in Devonshire was the excursion on 19 August to inspect the British Fleet anchored in Torbay; Joseph describes it to Antony thus:

> My Sister, Mr. & Mrs. Banfill & Bell[2] & myself have just made an excursion to Torbay to see the Fleet assembled there consisting of Ld Bridports & Ld Keith's Divisions, & amounting in the whole, the day we were there, to *50 Sail of the Line*. A day or two before there were collected together in the bay 55 Sail of the Line & 7 or 8 frigates. We set off on Monday Morning the 19th: the three Ladies in a Post

---

1. We owe the information in this paragraph to Dr. E. S. Leedham Green, Assistant to the Keeper of the Archives at Cambridge University Library.
2. Sibella Gibbs (1760–1841), Antony's unmarried sister.

chaise, & Banfill & myself on Horseback; we were luckily favoured with fine weather, we breakfasted at Newton Bushal,[1] & Dined at Tor Quay & while our Dinner was preparing we hired a Boat, & sailed round the Fleet: you may easily conceive it to have been the grandest sight of the kind ever seen, & certainly the most powerful Naval force ever collected together in the annals of Naval History: We returned to Exeter the same night highly delighted with the adventures of the Day. . . .

The remainder of the letter is less cheerful, being partly occupied with the financial embarrassments of John Hucks, and partly by the state of the nation and the conduct of the war:

. . . We have experienced a most dreadful season in this Country incessant wind & rains, which has done great & irreparable damage to the Hay, & the Corn; Every thing is uncommonly dear, & Coal scarcely to be had for money, the Government having impressed most of the Colliers & their crews for the service of the secret expedition, the first division of which amounting to 15,000 have been landed safely at Bremer Lee in the Weser. The remainder 20,000 more are about to follow. . . .

The letter was completed on 5 September with news of the British naval victory at the Texel:

. . . The Bells are ringing & ye Guns firing at this moment in a boisterous manner: The news is just arrived of our troops having made good their landing in Holland, at Halder (& not at Bremer Lee as above stated) that they have taken the Port of Halder[2] with the loss of near 500 killed & wounded; & a loss to the Enemy, of near 3 times that Number. & that in consequence of this victory, the *whole* Dutch fleet has fallen into our hands without firing a Gun; upwards of 20 Ships of war of various sizes; It appears from a very bold & gallant reply of Storer the Dutch Admiral to our Summons of Surrender 'that He & his brave officers would have fought for the only Sovereign He acknowledged, the Batavian Republic to the last extremity, but for the Traitors under his Command who refused to fight' The news of the *total Defeat* of Joubert's army & of the Death of that General is confirmed.[3] Would to God this hour of victory might induce a disposition for *peace* in *either* of the contending parties. . . .

Shortly after writing this letter, Hucks had the pleasure of renewing his acquaintance with Coleridge, who, in the course of a short visit to Southey at Exeter, dined at Cleave House, as Coleridge tells Poole in a letter dated 16 September:

1. Newton Bushel, once a small town just outside Newton Abbot, now part of it.
2. On 27 August 1799.
3. Joubert was killed at the Battle of Novi Ligure on 15 August.

. . . I have dined with a Mr. Northmore, a pupil of Wakefield's who possesses a fine House half a mile from Exeter—in his boyhood he was at my Father's School—& *my* Great Grandfather was *his* Great great Grandfather's Bastard but it was not this relationship however tender & interesting, which brought us acquainted—but Southey & self called upon him, as Authors, he having edited a Tryphiodorus & part of Plutarch & being a notorious Antiministerialist & Freethinker.—He welcomed us, as he ought to do—and we met at dinner Hucks, at whose House I dine on Wednesday—the man who toured with me into Wales & afterwards published his Tour—Kendall, a poet who really looks like a man of Genius, pale & gnostic, has the merit of being a Jacobin or so but is a shallowist and finally, a Mr. Bamfield[1]—a man of sense, information & various literature—and most perfectly a Gentleman—in short, a pleasant man. At his house we dine to morrow—Northmore himself is an honest vehement sort of Fellow, who splutters out all his opinions, like a Fizgig [a squib or firework] made of Gunpowder not thoroughly dry sudden & explosive yet ever with an adhesive Blubberliness of Elocution—Shallow, shallow—a man who can read Greek well, but shallow—yet honest, one who ardently wishes the well-being of his fellow men, & believes that without more Liberty & more Equality this Well being is not possible. He possesses a most noble Library. . . .[2]

Coleridge's letter would imply that he and Southey dined with Hucks on 18 September, but Mrs. Hucks's diary, according to J. A. Gibbs, records their visit as taking place on 11th.[3] That both dates fall on a Wednesday suggests that either Mrs. Hucks or Coleridge was a week out in the reference. Whenever the visit occurred, it was doubtless one of the occasions referred to by Southey when he wrote of Hucks at a time when he planned to include some of his poems in his *Specimens of the Later English Poets* (1807):[4]

I knew him & have past with him many pleasant & rememberable hours. He died in the prime of life, of consumption, the scourge of this country. . . .[5]

1. Samuel Banfill (see pp. xx–xxi above).
2. *Letters*, I. 528–9.
3. Gibbs, *History*, p.94 note.
4. See Raymond D. Havens, 'Southey's *Specimens of the Later English Poets*', *P.M.L.A.* LX (1945), 1066–79.
5. *Ibid*, p.1072. See also *New Letters* I. 228 and note. It is just possible that Southey also alludes to Hucks in a letter to Coleridge of 25 July 1801: 'Poor H-, he has literally killed himself by the law; which, I believe kills more than any disease that takes its place in bills of mortality . . .' (*The Life and Correspondence of Robert Southey*, ed. C. Southey, 1849, II. 152). It would seem that Grosvenor Bedford, Southey's co-editor, was responsible for the omission of Hucks's work from the *Specimens*.

In 1800 he printed three of Hucks's poems in the second volume of his *Annual Anthology* published in Bristol,—'On Viewing the Monastery lately erected at Lulworth', 'To a Flower', and 'To his Veil',[1] none of which had appeared in *Poems* (1798).

Southey and his wife seem to have dined at Lower Cleave again on 1 October, according to Mrs. Hucks's diary;[2] this may be the occasion alluded to in Southey's letter to Coleridge, dated 11 October:

> Will you believe? I converted Kendall to English hexameters, and he said it would do; and Banfill, whom I thoroughly astonished. Northmore had his quantity and his spondees so stuck in the mud of his brain that he could not get rid of them. He is an excellent man whom every body teaches me to esteem, but he has an obstinacy that would do honour to a pig. . . .[3]

Coleridge's reply of 15 October refers to the little group of Exwick friends:

> . . . It is singularly unpleasant to me that I cannot renew our late acquaintance in Exeter without creating very serious uneasiness at Ottery: Northmore is so preeminently an offensive character to the Aristocrats.—He sent Payne's [i.e. Tom Paine's] Books as a present to a Clergyman of my Brother's Acquaintance a Mr. Markes—this was silly enough.—Either however I will not visit Exeter, or I will visit Banfyl for I am much taken with him.—Did Hucks say aught of having received a letter from me, from Taunton, written on the same day on which we left Ottery?— . . .[4]

By this time Hucks was likely to have returned to London, Coleridge (probably on 11 or 18 September) having had him record his address as 9 Inner Temple Lane, in his notebook.[5] The date of the entry is, however, a matter of conjecture rather than proof. The first entries in the Gutch Notebook seem to date from early in 1795, the latest from late 1799 or early 1800. Hucks's earliest extant letters from 9 Inner Temple Lane date from the early summer of 1796, so that he could have recorded his address for Coleridge at any time between then and January 1800 when he moved to No. 4 Inner Temple Lane. The notebook does not seem to have been used during Coleridge's absence in Germany from September 1798 to July

1. *Annual Anthology*, Bristol, 1800, II. 50–2, 194, 196–7.
2. Gibbs, *History*, p.54 note.
3. *New Letters*, I. 201.
4. *Letters*, I. 540.
5. Now the Gutch Notebook (B.M. Add 27901.) See *Notebooks*, I. Entry 168 and note. Also Notes, pp. xix, xx. For comments on Hucks's address, see note 3, page xxvii above.

1799. Unfortunately there is no evidence that the Gutch Notebook accompanied Coleridge to Devonshire in September 1799 either, but it is hard to resist the view that this was the occasion on which the entry was made, a reunion between two friends being a likely moment for an exchange of addresses.

Only one other Hucks letter appears to date from 1799, that addressed to Antony Gibbs from Inner Temple Lane, but without a date (*FL* V. 439–42). It chiefly turns on public affairs, particularly parliamentary reform, and proceeds to a discussion of the necessity for a classical education, since at this time Antony was thinking of placing his second son William at the Charterhouse, and seeking his brother-in-law's advice on its academic merits.[1] Hucks begins by referring to the expiry of Antony's lease on Lower Cleave House:

> . . . Billy Pitt by Gods blessing may be hanged before that time and the Directory overthrown,[2] & Charles Fox *in*, & all the Blood hounds of every Denomination *out* . . . I am certain that our Lord the King, will retain Mr. Pitt as *his* Minister till his dying day, if he can; but I think the People will at last insist upon his dismissal; they are inexcusable for not having done it before, If there is a chance that a tollerable [*sic*] peace would be the consequence of a Change of Administration I cannot discover why that Chance is to be sacrificed to the interest of three of four individuals. With respect to the great questions of National Salvation; I am *still* of opinion, that the Country may be saved, provided a radical reform of every corrupted branch of Administration takes place, but not a corner must be left unsearched; Nothing but this will do; The most rigid economy must also be substituted in the Room of the most profuse & mad prodigality: No doubt Mr. Pitt will, if the Nation continues to repose that fatal confidence in him which they have hitherto *blindly implicitly* & *without the slightest enquiry* done, support by artificial operations of finance, our exhausted resources for a few years longer; but He can never *restore* the constitution to its positive vigour, & *practical* freedom, without a general Reform *in* & *out* of Parliament; and to use his own words, when he himself was in days of yore a Reformist 'Without a Parliamentary Reform no bad Minister can be ever responsible, nor can a good one be of any avail'.
>
> My opinions are much changed about the Utility of learning Latin & Greek at a public school; I do not think that such learning is entirely lumber; but I am persuaded the time which is spent in the acquirement of it, might be much more usefully employed; in

1. William Gibbs eventually attended Blundell's School, Tiverton. (See Gibbs, *History*, p.127).
2. The French Directory resigned on 9–10 November 1799, leaving the way clear for Napoleon to become First Consul. William Pitt remained in office until 14 March 1801.

studying the art of speaking composing & pronouncing well their own native tongue which is surely more of a National object than the learning to construe a page of Thucydides: An early knowledge of practical Philosophy, which would be opening a field for national discoveries in arts & sciences; There are very good translations of the antient writers from which they might learn the strange History of Man in all ages: And I contend, that in the time usually passed at a public school, *generally* in learning nothing at all; & *at the best*, but to acquire an imperfect knowledge of *two* dead languages; a boy might become a good proficient in practical Mathematics, which embraces almost every thing useful in Society with respect to the arts, and many with respect to the Sciences; He would learn his own language, with propriety, & be well versed in the living ones most adapted by men *out* of their own Societies, as French Spanish & Italian; & He would also be familiar with the Whole range of *modern* History. . . .

Hucks spent his final winter in London; on 13 January 1800 he told Antony Gibbs that he had 'opened Shop for myself as a Special Pleader'[1] and would thus be unable to leave London 'till ye middle or latter end of July'; he adds that he has recently moved into new chambers at No. 4, Inner Temple Lane. At the time his brother John's financial affairs were occupying a good deal of his thoughts and energies. A fresh hint of his fatal illness comes in a letter to Dorothea dated 12 March (*FL* V. 617–20) when, in the course of enquiring after her own poor health, he writes:

> . . . the truth is the late Season has been severe enough to kill a Rinoceros, much less would have sufficed for a Xtian—Do not think of writing or stooping, for tho' yr affect^te letters are amongst my greatest comforts, yet I will now willingly hear of you instead of from you. *I* know how detrimental stooping is to those who have any complaint upon their Chest. . . .

Whether it was because of this remark, or, as seems more likely, through some indiscreet revelation by Henry Towneley Ward, Dorothea evidently became alarmed enough about her brother's condition to make enquiries of Eleanora her sister, for on 17 March Joseph wrote again (*FL* V. 623):

> . . . I confirm what Mrs. Ward says (viz) that my Cough is by *no means* serious; a mere trifle that periodically attacks me for a short period every year, to prevent me I suppose from growing rather too presumptuous upon a continued series of good health: A happy return of fine weather, & a little Country air will I have no doubt speedily restore me to perfect health & its usual attendant insolence. By the

---

1. An advocate specializing in drawing up pleadings for use in court, and in attending Judges' chambers.

bye in yr next let me know, who told you ye long Cock & Bull story of Coughs, pains in ye Chest, & Consulting Physicians etc. . . .

Despite his own casual even flippant air, the Gibbs family letters leave no doubt that Hucks's state of health had often caused his mother anxiety; writing to Dorothea as early as 26 March 1785 (*FL* II. 313), she comments that

> Joseph is thin but hope his Cough is better & flatter my self it will continue so, as he is to go into College at his return to Eaton. . . .

Four years later she was more seriously alarmed, as a letter to Dorothea dated 16 September 1789 (*FL* III. 279–80) makes clear:

> Poor Joseph left me on Sunday & I'm afraid far from well; the Week before he went [i.e. back to Eton] he was very ill indeed, Heaviness, & drowsiness, in his head, Lassitude, lothing his Meat, & what he did take, came immedeately off his stomach and great difficulty in breathing which he frequently complains of. I spoke to Mr Gibbs [i.e. Antony] who advised bleeding, & an Emetic, the last he took, & was certainly better, but I have a thousand fears about him, as he keeps his complaints to him self, don't love to be thought ill, and if he could have kept himself up he would not have told me; but Mr. Bamfil had asked him to dinner at Exwick where with difficulty he got, but fell sick at the sight of the Meal & was carried up stairs to Bed. . . .

On 25 March 1800 Hucks wrote again, from 3 Henrietta Street, the Wards' London home, a long rallying letter mocking at Dorothea's fears for him (*FL* V. 627–30):

> My Dear Sister's discernmᵗ is truly astonishing, & her powers of seeing thro a shallow artifice equally a subject of admiration. I can see her triumph, at having so sagaciously unmasked the treacherous form of good health that I had so deceiptfully assumed; & tho I had ye cunning to convince all who surrounded me, talk'd with me, eat with me, touched me, & look'd at me, that my indisposition *was not serious*, yet She, at the distance of 175 miles, disdaining vulgar opinion, boldly pronounces it *serious*! I am much obliged to her for her decision, but with her leave I had rather wait a little longer, & commit ½ a dozen more follys, before any thing shall be serious that appertains to me. But what is to be done in the mean time? how convince this serious Sister of mine that my health tho not absolutely perfect is yet very well behaved & orderly? I have been meditating a thousand Schemes, & I verily believe I must come down to Cleve & convince her of it in propriâ personâ. . . .
>
> And now I will give you a faithful account of my complaint. As usual I was plagued with Colds my old Enemy ye whole Winter tho I assure you I took every care of myself that could be, & about a Month ago it degenerated into a Cough, upon perceiving which I *immediately*

confined myself & sent for an Apothecary; a Cough is not to be got under in an instant [.] I there continued neither better nor worse for a fortnight when Mr. & Mrs. Ward kindly pressed me to come here which I did the same day; here I got a little better, when upon Mrs. Ward's particular request I sent for Sir Walter Farquhar;[1] under his directions I have rapidly advanced towards a cure; & have no doubt that if I remained here or went into ye neighbourhood, in either case I shd soon recover; but Sir Walter is remarkable for caution, & being determined to make sure of my speedy reestablishment rather wishes me to go for a little time to a milder climate. This I have complied with to please him; & Indeed am almost glad that it has so happened, since I shall on this account so soon have ye pleasure of seeing you & my Dear Mother; for judge of my satisfaction, when on my hinting Exeter, He said it was as good a place as any I could go to; My stay with you will be guided by circumstances;

 Now My Dear Sister I hope I shall not hear of, or find you, when I come, ridiculously alarmed; excuse the term; but I *can* see no reason for falling into fears & apprehensions before one knows certainly *why* or *wherefore*. There is nothing extraordinary in a man having a Cough, nor any thing alarming, that to one who has a Cough Easterly winds & London Fogs should be unwellcome guests. I therefore hope my Mother & you will lay aside all suspicion, & we shall meet in Sunshine & not in *showers*. . . .

Dorothea Gibbs was plainly reassured by Joseph's letter, for she wrote to Antony in Lisbon on 27 March (*FL* V. 635–8):

. . . I am glad Joseph is coming to me, for I will so nurse him and myself that you shall see us quite strong and healthy when you come. . . .

But when Hucks arrived at Lower Cleave House on 9 April accompanied by his brother John, her worst fears seemed to have been confirmed; she wrote to her husband on the day of Joseph's arrival (*FL* V. 641–2A):

We left [for] Exwick last Friday as we expected poor Joseph every day, he arrived in Exeter with John last night, I will tell you how he is, when I see him, but I fear in a very weak state for they have been Eight days in coming from London, and they came in Chaises all the way, he staid two days at Bristol . . . I am glad that he is coming here as the air of Devonshire always agreed with him, and if care and attention will restore him he will not long be ill, John is this moment come in, he says his Brother is much better, but that he has been in a very dangerous way, he has still a bad Cough, and Night Sweats I am

---

1. A fashionable physician of the period, Sir Walter Farquhar (1738–1819) was created a baronet in March 1796, and in the same year became Physician-in-ordinary to the Prince of Wales, later George IV.

quite afraid of seeing him—he will be here soon in a chair, how my heart beats— . . . Joseph is just come, that is he has been here two hours he looks dreadfully, God grant he may get over it but I am sure he is far gone in a consumption—he is only a shadow of what he was in the Autumn when he left us [.] he is in tolerable Spirits, says he has not the least fear of himself—his appetite is too good, but he is not to eat any animal food—in May I hope I shall be able to get an Ass [?] for him—his Night sweats are very violent and so I think his Cough is but he says it is better, I find Sir Walter Farquar [sic] wishes him to try Lisbon if this air does not soon have a good effect. . . .

Antony Gibbs cannot have been much reassured by his brother George's opinion of Hucks's chances of survival, as conveyed in a letter of 13 April (*FL* V. 643–6):

He was exceedingly reduced in flesh, carried the appearance in his face of a person in an advanced stage of a consumption, of which I am very sorry to add that he had the symptoms that generally attend this disorder—night sweats, & a bad cough with feverishness at times— . . . it is certainly much to be feared that his disorder is too deeply fixt to be removed. . . .

Hucks's condition continued to deteriorate during the early summer of 1800; in June Dorothea accompanied her brother to the Hotwells in Bristol, in the hope that his discomfort might be eased, but George Gibbs informed Antony on 24 June that 'there is no amendment from which, I fear, any hopes of his recovery can be grounded' (*FL* V. 675–7).

And so it proved. Joseph and his mother proceeded from Bristol to Exmouth, where, acting on the advice of the Physician-Extraordinary to George III, Dr. Carmichael Smyth,[1] he seems to have spent as much time as possible sailing.[2] Towards the end of July the family correspondence is concerned with the possibility of obtaining a berth for Hucks on board a man-of-war, or a trip to Lisbon or to the West Indies, but time was growing short. It must have been apparent to all members of his family that, despite their solicitude and that of his doctors, Joseph was dying.

He died at Exmouth on 19 September 1800, and was buried in the

---

1. James Carmichael Smyth (1741–1821) was an eminent Scots physician and medical writer: he became a Fellow of the Royal Society in 1779.
2. See Richard Polwhele, *History of Devonshire*, 3 vols, 1797–93–1806: 'The air of Exmouth is, undoubtedly, favourable to persons labouring under consumptive disorders, especially those who have felt the first attack in an inland situation" (II. 216).

nearby parish of Withycombe Raleigh on 23 September.[1] George Gibbs wrote to console Antony on 20 September, and paid tribute to Hucks's fortitude and amiability:

> ... his great patience ... was the effect & completion of that character of mildness & sweetness of disposition which he always possessed, & having supported him thro' the last trying scene will no doubt find their reward with that all gracious Being who has called him hence. . . . (FL V. 723–4)

A little later Dorothea was to write to Antony

> Every day I think I feel the loss of my dearest Joseph more for he was always the same kind friend. . . .[2]

and from his letters Hucks emerges as a likeable and cheerful young man, an affectionate and dutiful son and brother, with a shrewd eye for the follies and frailties of his fellow-men. While his letters to his family abound in badinage and good humour, he was predominantly of a serious disposition and could wax sententious on occasion; as he once protested to his sister (8 October 1796) (FL IV. 475–8):

> ... You know that I was never addicted to Compliments, & never less disposed to make them than with those I love—And where I am most grave, it is always a sign that I am there most at home, for where I am grave I am always more myself & more comfortable—This is odd doctrine at least it would so appear to the generality of men who think it always necessary to have a grin upon their faces & a comp^t in their Mouths— . . .

Politically Hucks appears to have been an implacable opponent of the war policies of the Pitt Government, though the fact that he was not an extreme radical is illustrated by his remark on 25 November 1794, in a letter to his sister, concerning the acquittal of Horne Tooke[3] on 22 November on a charge of high treason (FL IV. 327–9):

> ... I was happy to hear Mr. H. Tooke is acquitted . . . not that I care

1. A transcript of the parish register is in Exeter City Library. The *Exeter Flying Post* of 2 October 1800 records the death thus: 'Lately died at Exmouth, of a decline in the 29th year of his age, Joseph Hucks, youngest son of Wm Hucks Esq. late of Knaresborough in Yorkshire'. We owe this and the preceding reference to Mr. G. P. Stone, Deputy City Librarian. The present incumbent informs us that the old parish church and graveyard at Withycombe Raleigh were closed over a hundred years ago, and a road and the premises of a school now cover the site.
2. Gibbs, *History*, p. 125. We have not located this letter in *FL*.
3. John Horne Tooke (1736–1812) was a leading English radical and a pioneering philologist. In 1794 he was committed to the Tower of London on a charge of high treason, it being claimed that the corresponding societies had as their aim the subversion of the constitution. He was acquitted after a trial of six days. Many of his remarks are to be found in Coleridge's *Table Talk*.

a farthing about Horne Tooke but I rejoice to find there was no such plot in existence as a design to overthrow the Government or indeed any *foundation* for those foul Calumnies thrown out by the Ministers against the best friend to the Constitution. . . .

It is difficult to form an estimate of Hucks' intellectual capacity, since so much of his life at Eton, Cambridge, and the Inner Temple remains a closed book to the researcher. The impression given by his letters is that of a diligent, painstaking, and assiduous mind rather than a brilliantly incisive or penetrating one, an assessment which the placement as a Junior Optime tends to confirm: it is undeniable that the tenure of an Oxford or Cambridge Fellowship in the late eighteenth century was not the mark of scholarly distinction which it is generally felt to be today. But the award of King's Scholarship to Eton, the ardent application to study and literary composition, and the evident erudition of the Northmore circle at Exwick suggests that Hucks could hold his own in the company of cultured and educated men. Furthermore, neither Coleridge nor Southey is likely to have sought Hucks's company merely on the grounds of his amiability; certainly, on the basis of the evidence here collected together, Joseph Hucks can be considered no unworthy companion to Coleridge on their pedestrian tour through North Wales.

II. *The Tour*

A Pedestrian Tour through North Wales, in a Series of Letters, is composed of seven letters addressed to an unspecified and thus unknown recipient; nonetheless, in the last letter Hucks expresses the hope and expectation of seeing him in Cambridge 'very soon', so we may assume he was a friend at Cambridge. The series of letters is a convenient narrative form particularly appropriate for travel journals although the form was equally well established as a form of fiction in the epistolary novel. The letter-form has, among other advantages, that of rapid assumption of intimate and personal relationship between writer and reader. Moreover, the form offers the writer limitless scope for the development of any and every idea that enters his head within this assumed framework of private relationships.

We can only regret that Hucks did not take full advantage of the freedom the form offers. In his preface he claims his reader's indulgence for 'tautology and egotism', but the work is not in fact particularly tautological, and unfortunately there is too little 'egotism'. A more immodest display of egotism would at least have enabled us to establish some picture of the author and to establish his book as autobiography. The strong impression gained is of a somewhat priggish young man more interested in opinions, however second-hand, than in first-hand experiences or ideas. A little less modesty would not have been out of place. Indeed, although Hucks clearly considered his radicalism a prominent feature of his adventurous views, his book is evidence of a rather conventional though restless and enquiring mind. It would be too obvious and quite unjust to say that both the tour and tourist were pedestrian though the temptation to do so is strong. The problem is Hucks's inability to define clearly his real objective. In attempting to describe in personal terms his walking tour through North Wales, he fails to be vividly personal enough, thus depriving us of that autobiographical element that might have enlivened a reader's interest. No doubt this is owing to his attempt to combine autobiography with the writing of a travel book, although the result may be judged lacking on both counts. The 'amusement of an individual was originally the sole object of the following letters,' he says in his preface, 'but he [the author] has ventured to make them public, under the hope that they may, in some measure, contribute to the satisfaction of those who have not seen, yet may wish to become familiar with, the outlines of a country, so dissimilar in every respect to England' (p. 2). He offers his book as a collection of descriptions, personal impressions and ideas as written by a friend to his friend, as an introduction to a strange land and people, and as a travel-guide 'to those who, like himself, might be induced to explore the beautiful scenery of North Wales' (p. 3). However, although he did not undertake the tour alone, he has, as he says, 'spoken of himself as being the only spectator'. Since Coleridge was his companion throughout the tour and since history, not without some good reason, is more interested in Coleridge than in Hucks, we can only regret that Hucks did not speak more of his companion or allow us to learn more about him from his book. Hucks's acknowledgement of a general debt to his fellow-travellers is too vague to be helpful; he is, he says, 'greatly indebted to them for many interesting remarks and useful information' and we cannot resist remarking that a more individual and precise account of these remarks and this information would have put Coleridge scholars more deeply in debt to him.

Nonetheless, so far as the composition of the book is concerned, we must assume either that he edited severely the letters he sent to his Cambridge friend or that his use of the letter form is a convenient fiction, a useful vehicle by means of which necessarily loose and heterogeneous materials are held together. Had he written actual letters to a real friend in Cambridge concerning a tour undertaken by himself and other Cambridge undergraduates, is it not likely that his whole tone and style would have been more relaxed and conversational, his comments more personal and more concerned with the personalities of the others? The very formality of Hucks's style and manner suggests that from the first he was addressing himself to a larger public, one often denoted by the term 'the gentle reader'. If there were letters originally, they are no longer extant but in any case it does not seem unduly rash to suppose that Hucks adopted the letter form as a literary device and that he wrote from the first with an eye to publication. The use of the letter-form for travel journals was, after all, a well-established literary convention.[1]

In his account of the tour Hucks subordinates, for the most part, his individual impressions and ideas in order to establish a general view. Although he deals with an interesting variety of subjects and records an impressive range of observations, first-hand response gives way to abstract speculations and everywhere particularities are polished to a smooth generality. He is aware of writing in the neo-classical tradition that does not concern itself with the streaks of the tulip. His style often betrays him and is mannered, knowing and self-consciously literary. Indeed, he is literary to a fault. Standing on the summit of Cader Idris, on the very edge of the 'precipice', he looked down 'into the frightful abyss of clouds' (pp. 51–2); oddly, he compares himself to Satan looking into Hell and finds the appropriate quotation from *Paradise Lost*, incorporating, presumably, the sublimity of horror. Similarly, on another occasion he notices that the Welsh children 'are remarkably beautiful, and usually well made', though from the age of ten onwards they begin to develop a 'haggard countenance, a reduced appearance, and, in short, all the traces of a premature old age' (p. 62). Apparently uneasy at asserting his own sharp observations on this phenomenon, he seeks support in a quotation from Adam Smith's *The Wealth of Nations*. It is as if Adam Smith's view that the mortality rate among the children of the Highlands is high not only adds credence to Hucks's own view of Welsh children but establishes it among those truths that are universally acknowledged.

In other words, what may at first seem a somewhat pedantic habit of quotation and cross-reference, a scholarly disposition, establishes itself firmly as a typical eighteenth-century mode. Essentially, of course, it is an attempt to achieve acceptable generalities, a determination not to see the trees for the wood, a limiting disability in a writer concerned with describing the features of North Wales. By

1. For example, Sterne's *A Sentimental Journey* is addressed to 'Eliza'.

concentrating their attentions on rural scenery, the Romantics weaned themselves away from the habits of generalization and learnt to particularize their experience by describing these same trees. By falling back continually, as if for reassurance and security, from acutely observed descriptions of people, places and events, to the familiarity of abstract, philosophical and literary ideas that seem to explain or at least contain them, Hucks betrays himself as an essentially eighteenth-century observer. In spite of his dismissive description of Pennant's *Tour in Wales* as a 'diffuse and voluminous work', it is clear that he had read it closely and is indebted to it for much of the information he incorporated into his own book. He is indebted to Pennant not only for antiquarian information concerning the places he visits but also for descriptions of local customs and even for the blind harpist singing in an inn—the blind harpist appears to be an obligatory figure in all early tourists' descriptions of Welsh life. In addition to reading Pennant, Hucks had clearly coached himself for the tour as for an examination by reading other relevant authors. He shows his classical Etonian pedigree by his references to Julius Caesar and Tacitus who shared unfounded views concerning the druids of Anglesey (Wordsworth was also familiar with these accounts of the druids). Hucks much admired the poet Thomas Churchyard, whose work he carried with him as 'a constant companion in my walks', and clearly the moralistic sixteenth-century generalities of his *Worthiness of Wales* (1587) refreshed the stock of quotations that Hucks was apparently accustomed to carry with him and to display on appropriate occasions. His book is prefaced by a quotation from James Beattie's Spenserian poem 'The Minstrel'; for storms, heights and the wilder aspects of feeling and thought he relied mainly on the sublimity of Milton and Collins; he could also rely for some support on Gray when considering the pestilence of war. His individual responses are either widened into generalities or filtered through his reading and in some cases his response is to his reading rather than to experience. Thus his reading of Churchyard confirms his view of the Welsh way of life as passed in amity and concord, courtesy and pride, industry and domestic virtue. At this remove in time we can only hope that the Welsh way of life was once all these things, though we now know that the pastoral life is more readily accessible in literature than in life, even Welsh life.

Historically speaking, Hucks's book is not without intrinsic interest in as far as it marks the transition between late eighteenth-century attitudes and the Romanticism that follows. Moreover, Hucks demonstrates just how smooth the transition really was for if,

xlii

by education and cast of mind, he demonstrates predominantly eighteenth-century attitudes, the interests that preoccupy him are those on which Romanticism is founded. For example, his faith in the natural goodness of man and the demonstrable benevolence of God is the basis of his radicalism, and his radicalism, however superficial, is by no means discontinuous with eighteenth-century rationalism and utilitarianism. If, therefore, he finds the 'noble savage' still alive and vigorous in the remoteness of North Wales, he uses this discovery as a means of overthrowing the old ghosts of atheists and Manicheans who still haunt his age. Rousseauesque natural man is pressed into service to strengthen the old arguments of the Leibnitzians. Near the beginning of his book and before he really starts his tour of North Wales, Hucks makes it clear that sunset and sunrise are decisive proof of God's benevolent existence, and his experiences in the wilds of Wales reinforce his conviction that natural man in the state of nature is naturally virtuous. Even his rhetoric has a familiar ring about it:

> Let the atheist or the *manicheist* (if such there are in reality, as I know there are some professedly), pay a little attention to the philosophy of nature, ever changing, but still connected, at once majestic but simple, disdaining the rules and frigid boundaries of art, at the same time modelled upon the most beautiful and graceful proportion—their short-lived doubts must instantly vanish, and their daring incredulity yield to the most rational and forcible conviction; they must then confess that this world could never have been created by chance, or be the work of a *malignant* deity; but that it bears the traces of a hand divine, the beautiful production of a benevolent, eternal, and intellectual being. I can scarcely believe there is that man existing, who can see without emotion the beauteous orb of day rising in the east, and in the evening behold its setting beams; who can look with apathy upon the moon when she gilds the brow of night, and all the numerous host of stars, the panoply of heaven, that shine around her; who equally unmoved by storms and sunshine, calms and tempests, can yet be induced, from a pitiful and weak despair of a happy futurity, from a wilful incredulity, or a misguided scepticism, to deny the great and generating cause of all effects! (p. 7)

Fundamentally, this is a neat summary of late eighteenth-century deism, however eclectic. The argument from effect to cause and in particular to the *primum mobile* is commonplace. Nonetheless, the confidence with which he brushes aside despair, incredulity and scepticism, replacing them with what he describes as 'most rational and forcible conviction', is breathtaking. Clearly his argument derives from something more than the notion of God as the necessary maker of the harmonious mechanism of man and universe. Hucks

xliii

has moved the argument of the first cause beyond Paley's analogy of God the watchmaker. Indeed, he has really moved the whole structure of the argument from the mechanical to the aesthetic while leaving the main argument intact. Art, he affirms, is governed by 'rules and frigid boundaries', thus confirming his basic neo-classicism, but God is the original genius, the supreme example of the sublime in poetry, who 'disdaining' the rules like Shakespeare, Spenser and Milton transcends all 'frigid boundaries' and creates a world of such original authenticity that all who experience it cannot help but be convinced of the supreme and benevolent genius of its creator. In terms of literature, we might say that Edward Young, Richard Hurd and Thomas Warton—and, of course, Longinus—have supplemented the earlier Aristoteleans to produce a theoretical framework within which the 'rules' dispute the foreground with the hardening conviction that the wilder, original genius of sublimity may well be superior to all boundaries of art. Hucks's own rhetorical poeticism, his vocabulary of 'beauteous orb', 'brow of night', 'setting beams' as well as his inversions ('hand divine', for instance), place him firmly on the side of sublimity. Hucks, therefore, represents a movement away from philosophical theology towards what might be called aesthetic theology, the term nature undergoing a significant change of meaning in the process. Nothing can be more certain than that by confronting man and nature in the wilds of North Wales, the meaning of these terms is significantly displaced from the position they occupy in the writings of, say Pope and Johnson.

The shift in the meaning of nature is a focal point in considering the movement towards Romanticism and Hucks considered the main objective of his tour to be an exploration of nature:

> The chief object of this expedition, and from which I hope to derive the greatest pleasure, is to explore the hidden beauties of nature unmechanized by the ingenuity of man; as well as to make some observations upon the human character under every different attitude it may assume; in short, to study nature in her works, and man in society. (p. 7)

Hucks has already made it clear that the study of nature is itself the revelation of God. He now affirms that nature is best studied in its wild form 'unmechanized by the ingenuity of man'. The antitheses of town and country, artificial and natural, mechanical and spontaneous, contaminated and pure, are all beginning to emerge in preparation for fully-fledged Romanticism; man creates the oppressive mills of the cities and God the free beauty of the countryside.

xliv

Hucks's expedition into the natural world of wild Wales is not only a revelation of its 'hidden beauties' but also a revelation of God. This, of course, is immediately relevant to Hucks's address to the 'atheist or *manicheist*' or at least to those who profess to be such. The central problem confronting eighteenth-century deists was the existence of evil. The 'natural' theologists tended towards the view embodied by Pope in his *Essay on Man* that all partial evil was 'universal good'. Yet such an explanation was much too facile to gain any widespread acceptance among the thinkers of the age. Johnson's review of Soame Jenyns's *Enquiry* is the classic destruction of this view. The existence of evil was a continuing problem to those who upheld the concept of a benevolent God; the Manicheans resolved the problem in one of the earliest Christian heresies, once adhered to by Augustine, by embodying evil as a principle in itself, while the atheists reacted by rejecting God entirely, the course chosen by Voltaire, for instance. Hucks resolves the problem by arguing that man is inherently virtuous and noble and that evil is an attribute of society, not of God. In other words, the fact that man did not realize the noble virtue of his nature could be accounted for by the mechanisms of a man-made society that deprived him of his goodness and happiness. Hucks associates evil not with supernatural powers but with the oppressive operations of social institutions. The problem of evil is thus secularized and in this guise is inherited by the Romantics. The fact that the poor are so manifestly deprived of happiness and oppressed by society gives radicalism its mainspring and its moral impetus. As Hucks observes:

> Under the pressure of poverty and misfortune, the mind oftentimes forgets its noble nature, and the proper degree of estimation with which it should regard its own existence . . . To remove then this evil, by doing away the cause of the complaint (viz. Oppression), would be a work well worthy the attention of every friend of mankind . . . A human being, as he comes originally from the hand of nature, is every where the same; the capacity of improvement, the talents and virtues which the mind is capable of acquiring and exercising, are to every state of society alike inherent. Surely then all must rejoice in the melioration of that state, since to contribute to its improvement is the noblest pursuit of individuals, and ought to be the sole end of all governments. . . . To say that the state of society cannot be improved, is either to assert its perfection, to confess that all exertions to improve that state would be vain, or that these political evils are either necessary or irremediable. To the first of these arguments, if they can be deemed worthy of such a denomination, there is no necessity to reply, because it carries with it its own conviction; and with respect to the last, no one will hesitate to pronounce it an impious reflection

upon the benevolence of the Creator, whose intention could never be to subject man to any species of political tyranny whatever; and well indeed might this fair creation and celestial harmony be called a Manichean system, or work of a malevolent being, if he could sanction upon this globe the detestable crimes, and abhorred impieties committed under the patronage, and often the immediate consequence, of vicious and corrupted governments; or if he could fix so narrow and confined a boundary to human happiness. (pp. 8–9)

It is useless and hardly relevant to comment that Hucks has really failed to understand the problem of evil and the discussion it gave rise to. We must accept that he, in common with other young men of his generation, was inspired in his reforming radicalism by the conviction of God's benevolence and the natural goodness of man which, he believed, followed inevitably from that conviction. To doubt that God intended man to be both virtuous and happy or to doubt that God made man equally capable of virtue and happiness whatever his social position, is to doubt the existence of God. The idea that social institutions are tyrannical is not in itself new or surprising though the notion that they are oppressive because they inhibit the development of man's natural goodness adds a fresh dimension to social thinking. The miseries of the poor were evident for all to see and the realization that this was not in the nature of things either necessary or desirable was widespread between the time of Swift and Johnson, for instance, both of whom were Tories rather than radicals. The idea of social mechanisms as oppressive and tyrannical begins to gain ground at the time of Hucks and as his argument makes clear, this notion springs from a firm belief in a benevolent deity who intended that the world should be organized in an harmonious way so that the talents, nobility and virtue in every man should be fully developed and completely realized. The roots of this radicalism are deeply embedded in religion. Although it is consistent with those ideas attributed to Rousseau and embodied particularly in *Émile*, it is not the product of Voltaire's rational anticlericism. We see Hucks arriving at the realization of natural goodness, and its corollary that man is born free but everywhere is in chains, from a traditionally religious standpoint. In considering the political views of the Romantics, we should bear in mind Hucks's brand of radicalism, however mild and conservative, for their revolutionary fervour with its fundamental rejection of social institutions and its belief in the innate potentiality for good in man clearly stems directly from the deism of their predecessors and is not some novel theory recently imported from France. Moreover, and this is important to explain the evangelical fervour with which the Romantics pursued their radicalism, its impetus and direction are basically religious not secular. Nonetheless, we should not overlook the aesthetic element in Hucks's theology for the Wordsworthian peasantry share the literary pastoralism of Hucks's Welshmen.

In view of the eighteenth-century character of Hucks's radicalism, it is with some satisfaction that it makes its first appearance in his first letter, dated 11 July 1794 and written in Bala, and concerns itself with the most characteristic eighteenth-century vice, the exploitation of the clergy. Hucks is disturbed by the extreme poverty of the curates he meets, not, he hastens to add, because he wishes 'to insinuate that there is any disgrace in poverty', but such poverty might bring religion into disrepute in the eyes of the common people. An incumbent or vicar might well receive five hundred pounds a year in tithes from two churches while the curate who serves them both is limited by an act of parliament to a salary 'within twelve and fifty pounds per annum'. In a footnote Hucks researches this point more fully and does indeed find a record of curates with large families and absurdly low salaries. Of ten curates in widely-spread Welsh parishes the highest paid is the curate of 'Benguiley and Bettus, Radnorshire' who with a family of nine children, receives a stipend of £35 per annum, while the lowest paid are the curates of 'Llanvair, Monmouthshire', who with a family of four children receives £13 per annum, and the curate of 'Abernorlish, Caermarthenshire' who has a family of eight children and receives only £18 per annum. Hucks's indignation seems well-founded: these salaries were indeed 'contemptible and insignificant'. Moreover, as Hucks points out, the salary ought to have been 'proportioned either to the duty performed, or the value of the benefice itself' (p. 13). Thus Hucks, in however modest a way, attacks an unjust act of parliament and strikes at the root of the church's establishment and at the same time establishes a relation between need, work and remuneration. Indeed, in the *Tour* he is quick to notice and sympathize with poverty wherever he meets it, although Coleridge's letter to Southey (p. 92 below) suggests that Hucks's personal conduct sometimes belied his ideals. However, Hucks never blames their poverty on the poor themselves, which is the more usual response of his age. Far from accusing them of being idle, shiftless, good-for-nothings, he notices the industrious character of the Welsh poor and praises them for their pride, their self-sufficiency and their hospitality. He lays the blame for poverty squarely on the shoulders of the government. His plan for increasing the prosperity of North Wales is, in fact, a prototype of many subsequent schemes urged by the Welsh themselves on successive governments up to the present

xlvii

day but adopted by none. Hucks found the inhabitants of North Wales characterized by 'poverty and wretchedness' (pp. 62–3), both of which he regards as 'too true indications of misery and want, and of an inferiority of condition, justifiable upon no grounds whatever, either of revealed religion or natural equity'. His appeal to religious morality and to natural justice is typical of him and his concern marks his own generosity of spirit. He traces the economic deprivation of North Wales to three separate sources, the historical circumstances that disinherited the Welsh, a geographical situation unfavourable to ordinary commerce and, most importantly, the mountainous terrain that prevents agricultural development and makes communications and transportation difficult. He notes that the

> population of North Wales, compared with its extent, is very trifling, and unequal. This may be accounted for from a long chain of causes, but chiefly from the continual state of discord and warfare, in which the chiefs and princes were always involved, until the final subjugation of Wales by Edward the First, and even then, the inhabitants were treated merely as a conquered people, and admitted to few privileges of the conquerors; for it was not till the time of Henry the Eighth, that they were suffered to have the same advantages with English subjects. Secondly, from the situation of the country, which is too remote for the English land trader, and opposed to a very dangerous sea; added to which its ports are by no means so commodious and safe as those of England. Thirdly, and principally, the barrenness of the soil, together with the mountainous nature of the country, and consequently the great difficulty of land carriage, which is the chief obstacle to its internal trade. (p. 63)

Having described the problems and their causes which certainly are, as he says, 'serious impediments to the flourishing state and prosperity of the people', he nonetheless believes they 'are not beyond a remedy'. Indeed, he calls the government's attention not only to the seriousness of the situation but to the realization that it is their clear duty to improve it, arguing that if Attica could be transformed from a desert into the garden of Greece, the British government could do something to help the people of North Wales:

> it ought to become the duty of the legislature to provide every possible means of improvement, and to endeavour, by wisdom and attention, to remove or diminish those local inconveniences which are a bar to the happiness of the society of any particular district or tract of land over which that legislature has dominion: establish manufactures, hold out rewards for agriculture; in short, increase the population of the country by the most approved methods; wealth will follow of course, commerce will be extended, and the now desolated mountains

of North Wales may, at least, repay the labour of cultivation, though they can never be so productive and flourishing as those of their southern neighbours. (pp. 63–4)

Although Attica was transformed from desert, and 'Czar Peter' in turning Russia from a land of poverty and desolation into a great and flourishing empire faced greater and 'almost insurmountable obstacles', Hucks realizes that his appeal to the British government to intervene on behalf of North Wales will be ignored, as have similar appeals in the more recent past. He feels that governments by their very nature are insensitive to the needs of the governed and incapable of wise action:

> the sole end of governments seems to be forgotten, and, instead of having for their great and ultimate object, the happiness and advantage of that society by whom they were instituted; they now seem calculated only for the advantage of a few; and the legislators of nations are become the individual brokers of public property; which, with the lives of mankind, are squandered away, as ambition or caprice may rule the hour, and dictate to their councils. (p. 64)

This is lucid and pungent rhetoric in the best tradition of eighteenth-century political commentary. The fact that it is deployed on behalf of the people of North Wales underwrites both its sincerity and Hucks's disinterested spirit of radicalism. Hucks's style at its best is balanced, pointed and direct, and at all times it is adequate to the need to convey the restless, inquiring curiosity of his mind, but it is never so forceful as when he is expressing opinions concerning man and society. His response to landscape and scenery is always ambiguous and often dismissive; he is always more aware of his own memories and moods than of the scene before his eyes.

He remained rather unimpressed with mountains though he recognized them as prominent features of the North Wales landscape. His visit to Snowdon was a disappointment. He and his companions travelled from Caernarfon to Beddgelert, which he describes as 'a small village, or rather hamlet, situated at the foot of some prodigious high mountains', and at eleven o'clock at night in rain and storm, they set off to find the guide's house. After some difficulty, they found the guide, 'a good-looking lad about 17 years of age', named 'Ellis Griffith', who persuaded them 'with many weighty reasons' against climbing the mountain in that weather and at that time of night. Hucks and his companions spent the night in the guide's house though while they slept, he stayed awake poring over an old Welsh dictionary, comparing himself to Brutus in his tent at Philippi, listening to the storm and the waterfall outside and contemplating 'with a mixture of awe and surprise' the speed with which the human mind accustomed itself to strange and frightening circumstances. He woke everyone at four in the morning but because he was suffering from a cold and had no real inclination to proceed, his companions climbed the mountain without him while he returned to the inn at Beddgelert to await impatiently for their return. Their climb he describes as 'a fruitless and fatiguing expedition' for when they arrived at the summit of Snowdon 'they could see nothing but the impenetrable clouds, that almost constantly envelope these huge mountains'. As Hucks was the only member of the party not to climb the mountain we know with certainty that Coleridge did make the ascent, and we may recall what visions Wordsworth saw on the summit of Snowdon enshrouded in cloud, having followed the same path to the top accompanied by Robert Jones and the guide.[1]

Clearly Hucks felt he had missed nothing by not climbing Snowdon but he did manage the ascent to the top of Cader Idris. Carrying 'ham, fowl, bread and cheese, and brandy', the travellers began the three-and-a-half hour journey to the top of the mountain only to find that summit also surrounded by cloud and their view limited to less than fifty yards. Not only did Hucks not enjoy the occasion, he actually seems to have suffered a vision of Hell. Delight in climbing mountains was clearly initiated by the Romantics and its pleasures were hidden from their immediate predecessors. What little pleasure Hucks derived from his climb was purely incidental. He felt he had compensated to some extent for not having climbed Snowdon as he assures us that the height of Cader Idris 'is little inferior to that of Snowden'. (p. 52) Also he had the satisfaction of mocking the Welsh guide's superstitious belief that the giant Idris had actually slept on the mountain. As the mountain is actually called Cader Idris—Idris's Chair—at least the guide's superstition was embodied in myth and he quite properly rebuked Hucks for laughing at this time-honoured legend. (p. 60) Moreover, the experience on the mountain gave Hucks an opportunity to question the biblical story of the flood, a story which in his view could not adequately explain the formation of large masses of such height. He much preferred to believe that when God had completed the creation of the world from raw materials he did not quite know what to do with the rubbish that remained so he merely 'threw it together in various heaps of different magnitudes, just as it happened, and thus formed what we call mountains'. (p. 53) Clearly Hucks did not much care for mountains but his concept of them as heaps of

1. *The Prelude* XIV. 1–129. See p. lxvii below.

1

rubbish is neither perceptive nor romantic. It is, of course, honest and original, and also serves to remind us just how recent in the history of taste the enthusiasm for mountains really is.

There is no doubt that Hucks is typical of his age in the discomfort he felt when confronted with the more dramatic elements of the North Wales landscape. He much preferred the gentler, more domesticated landscape of the foot-hills and coastal plain to the harsh, frightening grandeur of Snowdonia. Like so many men of his age he liked to feel that he was totally in command of the landscape he inhabited. The wild, rugged, desolate heights of the Snowdonia range inspired him only with fear; he could not submit to the elements of nature when they presented themselves in such uncompromising terms. Indeed, in these forms, they were a threat to his very security. He liked scenery that organized variety in soft and harmonious patterns and presented itself as pleasing, charming and restful; of the landscape between Pont Aber Glaslyn and Tan-y-Bwlch, he writes:

> I am delighted with the situation, which is the most retired and pleasing I have ever seen; it stands upon the borders of a valley sufficiently high to command a view of its whole extent; the Druryd, a small, but interesting stream, winding its solitary course, undisturbed, through the midst of it; and, at the lower extremity, a simple, but elegant bridge, terminates the view. The woods are very picturesque, and cover the opposite hills to a great extent; gratifying the eye with a constant variety. (p. 47)

Hucks himself introduces the word 'picturesque' to describe these scenes, though fundamentally he admired the orderly, domesticated grace of such a landscape. Such scenery is viewed by him, of course, as conducting itself as an attractive, graceful and well-bred young lady. Moreover, it is also clear that he takes something of a voyeur's pleasure in such spectacles and wishes they could be viewed by a wider audience. It is as if he wants to parade something so pleasing before his fellows and invite them to share the pleasures of his own response:

> Why, my dear friend, has nature placed her most alluring haunts, her most delightful scenes, so far from the reach of man? Why has she prodigally squandered away upon so many distant and uncivilized regions, and upon this favoured country in particular, all her majesty and simplicity? Why has she given to a people, who behold, without enjoyment, scenes of beauty, where, for my part, I could be almost content to pass through this strange scene called life, in peace and solitude? I know you will blame me for thus giving way to visions, which ought not to be realized, and your answer I already anticipate

li

(viz.) that man was not made for solitude, or selfish enjoyments. (pp. 47–8)

Hucks, always sociable, assumes that man is essentially clubbable; his regrets that such beauty is wasted in places not readily accessible to others and on those in whom familiarity has bred indifference are familiar eighteenth-century views. They are, of course, attitudes that, even while Hucks was writing, Wordsworth was reversing; the love of solitude, the moral strength that accumulates to those brought up in the remote beauty of the Lake District and an admiration for the soft, feminine landscape of valleys in conjunction with the harsh, masculine grandeur of mountains are the foundations of his poetic, and it is Wordsworth's rather than Hucks's view that we inherit. This is not, of course, to suggest that landscape is properly seen in sexual terms, masculine mountains and feminine valleys, or that either Hucks or Wordsworth was aware that such attitudes were even possible. Both of them, however, were fully aware that their responses to landscape were not merely of the eye but evoked psychological, moral and philosophical areas of contemplation; both were aware of landscapes of the mind as well as landscapes in nature although only Wordsworth was able to establish a fundamental connection between them. For the most part Hucks, always contemplative, though seldom very penetrating in his thinking, is content with descriptions of this kind:

> . . . we had ascended a very high hill, when the vale of Clwyd, in all its beauty, unfolded upon the sight; it appeared like a moving picture, upon which nature had been prodigal of its colours. Hamlets, villages, towns, and castles, rose like enchantment upon this rich carpet, that seemed covered with wood and enclosures; in the midst of it, at the distance of about five miles, the town of Ruthin, partially appeared from the bosom of a most beautiful grove of trees; the vale on each side being bounded by a chain of lofty mountains, and far off, on a bold and rugged promontory, stood Denbigh with its strong fortress, the undisputed mistress of this extended scene. (p. 20)

Here, even the picture of Ruthin with its bosom of trees, twin vales and heavy necklace of mountains, is hardly memorable or, indeed, more than conventionally sketched in rather well-worn metaphors. As we have noted, Hucks's ideas, generally speaking, are more interesting and very much more striking than his descriptions of the scenes that give rise to them. Walking towards Llangollen, for instance, he discusses what he sees to be the traffic between the senses and the mind, and we must agree with him, in his habit of introspection, that his mind is better trained than his eye:

lii

The face of the country now became more interesting. The scene gradually assumed a less rugged appearance; the dark brown mountain, and the desolated heath, softened by distance, formed a beautiful contrast to the wild and irregular scenery that succeeded. We felt our spirits, which had before been depressed from the barren and gloomy country we had traversed, now much exhilarated, and we seemed to breathe a freer air. (p. 16)

The change of scenery from one kind of landscape to another, Hucks writes, is accompanied by an analogous change in the state of mind of the traveller; this interchange between the physical and mental state leads him to conclude that

There is an analogy in nature throughout, from the most torpid state of vegetable existence to the most refined subtlety of animal life; and he who has not considered this attentively, will be surprised, upon reflection, to perceive that his own self importance is solely derived from the contemplation of external objects; for deprive him of these, shut him out from nature, suppose him to be totally unacquainted with the harmony of this beautiful sphere, he must consider himself in the most contemptible point of view, created for no purpose, endued with powers of perception and reasoning for no possible good; his would be a mere comfortless state of existence, with a mind that could have no adequate idea, if any at all, of the deity; his would be a situation unworthy the character of his species, and little elevated above the brute creation. Certainly there is a chain of causes and effects throughout every creative world, whether mineral, vegetable, or animal; and all has an effect upon the mind of man. When we approach a desolate and cloud-capt country, an uncultivated and dreary scene, what is the cause that we frequently feel a damp upon our spirits? Why does it affect the mind, as it were, with a leaden weight, and depress the active springs of the imagination? It is from the analogy which nature, under every form she may assume, bears to the varied life of man. Memory backward turns her view, and assimilates the objects before her, to some certain passage of our life, that impresses upon the mind a shade of melancholy or joy, according as those passages may have been marked with pleasure, or with pain. It is not therefore that there is any absolute impression made upon the mind, from the scene before us, whether it be bright with sunshine, or overcast with clouds, but it is memory which associates to it some event, or transaction of former years, which, though scarcely perceptible, is the cause of such an effect. (pp. 16–17)

This passage is worth quoting at length because it is just such a discussion of perception, memory and imagination that lies in the centre of Romanticism. This is the theme taken up and developed by Coleridge in his poems and in *Biographia Literaria* and in Wordsworth, particularly in *The Prelude* and poems such as *Tintern Abbey*.

Indeed, many of Coleridge's poems such as 'The Eolian Harp' or 'Frost at Midnight' might well be considered as meditative poems that extend and develop the ideas here put forward by Hucks. It would, in fact, be very interesting indeed to know how far Hucks was indebted to Coleridge's conversations for the ideas he expresses, for basically the whole tenor of this passage is heavy with recognizably Coleridgean preoccupations. Starting from a commonplace, that our moods seem consistent with our surroundings, that sunny weather is cheerful and rainy weather depressing, Hucks gradually involves us in metaphysical ideas of much more significant application; to be deprived of the world of sense perception is to lose all sense of the self as an inner reality as well, of course, as losing all sense of the external world, including the sense of God. The interaction between the outer and inner worlds is dependant upon the relation between man and the whole created universe, 'mineral, vegetable, or animal', for man is an integral part of that world. The 'active springs of the imagination' can be released only if man is in a state of harmony with the world of nature; such is that state of 'joy' that Coleridge judged to be a necessary condition for the workings of the creative mind. Perception of the outside world is never, however, uninfluenced by memory and the power of memory is such that it may transfigure the world of perception according to previously established patterns of association. If Hucks were not found to be echoing Coleridge's ideas, it would be most surprising. So much so that we might then begin to wonder whether Hucks had any discernible influence on Coleridge's intellectual development. If Hucks is summarizing Coleridge's conversations, and this seems most probably the case, we could only wish that he had done so more precisely and at much greater length. How far is it, in fact, from ideas of this kind to a conception of

> the one life within us and abroad
> Which meets all motion and becomes its soul[1]?

We know the rôle played by memory in the act of perception worried Coleridge and probably is not fully defined within the context of the romantic imagination until Wordsworth embodies it in *Tintern Abbey* and *The Prelude* where it acts in a redemptive capacity. We recall that Wordsworth had the benefit of Coleridge's highly original thinking on the whole vexed question of perception and that Coleridge worked his way through Hartley's theories of association before arriving at his own influential conclusions.

Whether Hucks ever really understood the implications of what he

1. 'The Eolian Harp,' lines 26–7.

wrote here, we cannot tell. We can only say that we have no evidence in his writings to suggest that he did. He did, of course, understand that perception can influence states of mind and that states of mind may influence perception. Certainly he sees gloom and desolation in unlikely places so, perhaps, we might conclude that he was influenced in these instances by a gloomy and desolate state of mind. He is surprisingly impressed by the copper mines of Anglesey and considered them 'uncommonly grand and striking'. Looking down into the 'yawning chasm' of the mine he is reminded of the 'infernal regions' as, we remember, he was reminded of Milton's Hell when looking into the clouds from the summit of Cader Idris (on Anglesey his hell is classical, 'the pit of Acheron'). If we are surprised that he found Parys Mountain's copper mines impressive, he is surprised that Anglesey is called the granary of Wales for, he says, 'it appeared to us as one continued picture of desolation'. Yet Anglesey would seem to fit perfectly Hucks's own prescription for a beautiful, picturesque landscape with the correct balance of harmonious variety and without undue harshness; even contemporary tourists from the Home Counties have found Anglesey charming and agreeable. In Hucks's case we can only conclude that some unpleasant memories had intervened between perception and his state of mind.

There is surprisingly little eighteenth-century antiquarianism in Hucks's account of his travels and this is in itself refreshing. Except where he calls on Pennant's help, as, for instance, in explaining the 'miracles' associated with St. Winifred's Well at Holywell, he has little of his own antiquarianism to add. He does, however, describe one scene in Denbigh Castle that deserves to be better known as a classic example of the 'gothick'. He describes Denbigh Castle, with some justice, as 'more of a venerable, than a magnificent ruin' (pp. 21–2), and goes on to say how he amused himself by wondering about it, listening to two gentlemen quoting Shakespeare to each other with appropriate declamations and gestures, one of whom retired to a convenient spot and played on his flute 'the tender air of *Corporal Casey*'. Such antics clearly destroyed the appropriate mood for Hucks so he left the castle but when he returned all was silence again and he experienced something of the authentic 'gothick' *frisson*:

> nothing could be more awfully grand, than the scene before me, which I surveyed with a degree of admiration, not totally destitute of a superstitious fear. The venerable appearance of the whole fabric; walls, and battlements, rising in ruined majesty; broken arches, half covered by the creeping ivy, and enchanters night-shade, high gothic

windows, which but displayed the horrible gloom that reigned within; the mouldering tower, shook by every storm, affording an asylum to the owl, the bat, and the raven, lone tenants of these desolate mansions; whilst the moon bursting from a dark cloud, threw a partial gleam upon the pile, and served, by its feeble light, to discover the deep gloom of the remoter parts. At the same time, a fearful stillness every where prevailed, except that it was now and then interrupted by low solemn sounds of wind, that seemed to sigh amongst the distant turrets; the intermediate pauses impressing upon my mind a mixture of awe and veneration, which the surrounding scenery greatly contributed to encrease. (p. 23)

Hucks was moved enough by the experience to compose a poem, in blank verse of Miltonic resonance, 'Upon the Ruins of Denbigh Castle'. Apart from the absence of graves and ghosts, Hucks's description provides the perfect scenario for the gothic imagination to work in. Fortunately he provides surprisingly few set-pieces in the account of his tour, but we are particularly grateful that he retained this one. He makes more or less perfunctory use of historical information concerning castles and buildings of interest. For example, he includes a very brief summary of the history of Beaumaris Castle followed by a complaint that it has been repaired with barbarous carelessness and that the local people have made a bowling-green inside its walls.

On his journey from North Wales to the West Country, Hucks visited Tintern Abbey and gives a vivid impression of the approach to it through the Wye valley:

Ragland castle is a very fine ruin, belonging to the duke of Beaufort; the road from thence to Tintern, would gratify the most romantic imagination; the last three miles, or more, being a continual descent through a deep and gloomy wood, till the astonished traveller bursts from the surrounding scenery full upon the Wye, that rolls its muddy waves in rich meanderings through this solitary glen. The lively picture that immediately offers itself to the view, of boats in full sail, of others landing their cargo, with the busy and cheerful cries of the sailors and workmen, was like the effect of enchantment, and almost created in me an imagination, that I had arrived in another world, and had discovered a new order of beings. At some distance stands the abbey . . . (pp. 56–7)

This impression is followed by a history of the abbey and the 'suppression and overthrow of these seminaries of bigotry and superstition' (i.e. Roman Catholicism) by Henry VIII. Yet clearly it is the human scene that seizes Hucks's imagination. The boats in full sail, the cargo being landed, the busy noise of the sailors and workmen act on him like an enchantment, transporting him to a sense of another world, a feeling of having discovered another order of beings. The scenery would gratify the 'most romantic imagination' but Hucks's most vivid response is to the scene of busy, lively humanity. Wordsworth had first visited this same spot in the previous summer; he too had little enthusiasm for ruins or antiquarianism. The memory of his visit stayed with him vividly alive in his memory for five years until he again saw the Wye in company with Dorothy. Moreover, Wordsworth also felt the experience belonged to 'another world', the memory of which was a constant source of refreshment to his spirit,

> oh! how oft—
> In darkness and amid the many shapes
> Of joyless daylight; when the fretful stir
> Unprofitable and the fever of the world
> Have hung upon the beatings of my heart—
> How oft, in spirit, have I turned to thee,
> O sylvan Wye! thou wanderer thro' the woods,
> How often has my spirit turned to thee!

Neither in recalling this early visit, or in describing his visit five years later, when, of course, his poem was written, does he mention the busy commerce on the Wye. Indeed, he seems to have deliberately omitted this feature of the scene which Hucks so enthusiastically describes. It is important to bear Hucks's description in mind, therefore, when reading Wordsworth's poem if only to remind ourselves that *Tintern Abbey* is not primarily a topographical poem.

If Hucks's antiquarian interest is somewhat half-hearted—Pennant had worked this subject over thoroughly in writing of Wales—his interest in ideas does not diminish. He is, in any case, more concerned with people than with buildings or landscape. He is remarkably sympathetic to the Welsh and, for someone just touring the country for the first time, shows a real insight into the Welsh situation. His admiration for Caernarfon Castle is balanced by his realization that it stands both as a 'noble and magnificent' presence and as a symbol of tyranny and oppression:

> Of all the ruins which Wales has yet presented to me, the castle of Caernarvon is the most noble and magnificent. 'Vast as the pride of its founder', it evinces the warlike and invincible genius of the first Edward, of whose military prowess this country, as well as Scotland, furnish such numerous and melancholy proofs. Thank heaven, these fabricks of despotism are at length either levelled with the ground, or present a memorable lesson to mankind of the futility of human ambition.
>   This castle was erected in order to secure the passage into the Isle of

Anglesea, and to curb the people of the mountains, where the brave and hardy Britons had taken refuge from their insulting conquerors, resolved to prefer freedom and independance to ease and servitude. The eldest son of Edward was born here, and he was presented to the Welsh as their future prince. Such enormous buildings, abstractedly considered, excite only my abhorrence; . . . (p. 42)

Hucks was clearly aware of Thomas Gray's Pindaric ode 'The Bard' and, indeed, when visiting Conwy cannot resist the temptation to quote the description of 'Conway's foaming flood' without, apparently, realizing that Gray was referring to a point much farther up the river Conwy (probably near Betws-y-Coed) or noticing that Conwy at its mouth can by no stretch of poetic licence be described as 'foaming'. In poems such as 'The Bard', 'The Triumphs of Owen', and the posthumously published 'Extracts from *The Gododdin*', Gray not only embodies what his successors came to regard as touchstones of sublimity but also became one of the first to draw attention to the matter, history, language and culture, of Wales. 'The Bard' was received with some perplexity by Gray's contemporaries mainly because of what they felt to be its obscurities, particularly the obscurities of its allusions. Johnson's response was both typical of him and of his contemporaries when he asserted that 'to select a singular event, and swell it to a giant's bulk by fabulous appendages of spectres and predilections, has little difficulty; for he that forsakes the probable may always find the marvellous'.[1] Nonetheless, poetry that is condemned as difficult by one generation is often taken up with enthusiasm and read with ease by the next, sometimes precisely because their elders have judged it difficult. Certainly, there is no doubt that those of Gray's readers who were best fitted to admire the skill with which he mastered the intricate difficulties of the Pindaric ode in English were those least likely to understand the poem's subject or allusions. Although, of course, Gray never visited North Wales—he did visit Scotland and the Lake District—he did, with the help of the blind harper John Parry and, later, of the Rev. Evan Evans, a Denbighshire curate, take a scholarly interest in Welsh and the metrics of Welsh verse. John Parry had already edited several collections of Welsh music when Gray heard him in Cambridge and was sufficiently inspired by his 'ravishing blind Harmony'[2] to complete 'The Bard' which he had neglected for almost two years. The poem itself does not, in fact, mention Caernarfon Castle but associated as it is with Edward I and

1. *Lives of the Poets, Thomas Gray.*
2. See letter to Mason, 24 (or 31) May 1757, *The Correspondence of Thomas Gray*, ed. Paget Toynbee and Leonard Whibley, 3 vols, Oxford, 1935, II. 501–3.

his son, the first Prince of Wales, Hucks could hardly have resisted recalling this poem to mind. In Gray's poem the last of the Welsh bards defies Edward I and prophesies the eventual extinction of Edward's line and the restoration of a British king—with Henry Tudor—before hurling himself into the Conwy. Hucks's belief that the Welsh were the original inhabitants of Britain and that they had been tyrannously oppressed by Edward, symbolized by the ruins of Caernarfon Castle, was a response well-prepared for by Gray and others and developed by the Romantics from Blake onwards. Nevertheless, even if Hucks's attitude has been conditioned by his reading, it was also reinforced by his firm beliefs and no less genuine for all that.

We have, similarly, no reason to disbelieve his assertion that he was deeply affected by Welsh harp music (his liking for the music of the Irish bagpipe is more difficult to accept). Yet clearly it is the rustic simplicity of what he clearly believes to be a more natural, more innocent state of artistic expression that moves him most:

> It afforded me a satisfaction I had never before experienced, to find myself amongst a people, who act with all the simplicity of nature; totally destitute of the assumed appearance, and artificial manners of more modern times. The Welsh musick assimilates to the genius of the people, and is in general wild and irregular, but often plaintive, and always affecting; for the harp is perhaps more calculated to express the extremes of passion than any other instrument; it is astonishing with what skill and execution it is sometimes played upon, and with what enthusiasm the country people listen to it; (p. 18)

The whole scene of music and dancing transported Hucks and

> brought back the pleasing recollection of those happy ages, when riches and luxury had not corrupted the heart of man; but when all mankind were brothers, and the interest of one became the interest of all. (pp. 17–18)

In this description Hucks deliberately balances the Augustan world of control and order against the 'wild and irregular' genius of the Welsh people; but he goes much further in setting one value-system against the other, the past against the present, innocence against corruption and experience. The golden age of brotherhood has degenerated into the artificial, self-interested, unfeeling world of money and luxuriousness. Hucks's vision of natural man, living in a prelapsarian community of harmony finds its expression here, and is the exact reverse of all those values that he felt to be operating in the urban society he knew best. Enthusiasm, simple emotions and the extremes of passion are invoked with more confidence than nostalgia for remote 'happy ages'. Hucks positively affirms the world of natural man and confronts the corrupted heart of contemporary man not merely with a sense of lost innocence but with an entire loss of direction. He is particularly fond of the banal idea of life as a voyage; he might have done better to consider the truism that travellers in a strange country generally learn more about themselves than they ever do about the country through which they travel. Hucks, in describing North Wales, is particularly self-revealing; in travelling most see only what is already in their minds. Although there is no evidence to show that he was ever a Pantisocrat (see p. xvii above), we cannot help but conclude that during his whole tour he was fired with enthusiasm for Coleridge's idealist concept of the Utopian society and found abundant evidence in Wales to support the view that contemporary society was viciously corrupt and could be reversed only by a return to the original, 'natural' state of society. The idea of a wholly benevolent society seems, after all, a necessary corollary to his concept of a benevolent God. Yet even natural man must draw the line somewhere, for Hucks seems more shocked than delighted when at Abergele he found men and women bathing in a state of nature:

> . . . the inferior orders of people commonly bathe, without the usual precautions of machines or dresses; nor is it singular to see ten or a dozen of both sexes promiscuously enjoying themselves in the lucid element, regardless, or rather unconscious, of any indecency. Not being myself accustomed to this mode, I chose to retire farther up . . .
> (p. 29)

Hucks, confronted with natural man in a state of nature, could only admire and do otherwise. In spite of his enthusiasm for the prelapsarian ways of the Welsh, he always observes the proprieties and decorum of his education and background, however corrupted he may judge them to be. Even in this he is not untypical of his generation. We recall that before setting up the utopia of Pantisocracy on the banks of the Susquehanna, Southey insisted that the members of the new society should be respectably married according to the proper rites. Inconsistency is, of course, typical of every generation, particularly the inconsistency between belief and behaviour, though the gap is always widest in periods such as the 1790s in Britain where intellectual and moral revolution is entirely dissociated from any comparable social revolution. The young men of that period such as Hucks and Coleridge enjoyed the luxury of indulging their visions of a world in which liberty, fraternity and equality reigned without suffering any of the social upheavals that accompany such dreams when translated into social action. The

French were suffering these upheavals on their behalf, so to speak.

Despite the fact that France declared war on England in 1793, the young English radicals of 1794 were still able to dissociate themselves from the war and the government's actions. The impetus of the original ideals of the revolutionaries had not yet been lost in disillusion. Indeed, on several occasions in his account of the tour, Hucks is rather proud of having been mistaken for a Frenchman. Moreover, although he is careful to see that nothing he says can be interpreted as seditious, he leaves the reader in little doubt that he feels England is engaged in an unjust war, the tyrant oppressor against those who sought liberty and natural justice. The ambiguity surrounding the incident in the inn at Bala is an indication of Hucks's understandable fear of being accused of sedition. Coleridge in a letter to Southey dated 13 July [1794] and one to Henry Martin dated 25 July, states that the fracas in the inn was occasioned by his toasting General Washington and Joseph Priestley respectively. In Hucks's version, the toast proposed is to General Washington but he makes it clear that it was not proposed by either himself or Coleridge but by 'one of our neighbours at the other table'. (p. 14) It seems reasonable to assume that Coleridge did in fact propose a republican toast—though whether to Washington or Priestley even he cannot recall—but that Hucks attributed this to some third party in order to protect Coleridge. The clergyman in Bala was no doubt expressing the popular sentiment of the day when he replied to the toast with 'may all *Demicrats* be *gullotin'd*' and a year later, when Hucks's tour was published, popular support for the war against France was much stronger. Hucks is content, therefore, to mock the clergyman's accent and question the grounds of his sentiment while dissociating himself and Coleridge entirely from the incident. Indeed, in his book Hucks retained only one explicit outburst of indignation against the war. At Holywell, a once thriving town which 'is now', he says, 'forsaken for the sword' he refers to

> numbers of poor women and children, who are half starving, whilst their husbands, fathers, and brothers, are gloriously signalizing themselves in the service of their country; and if by chance the ruthless sword of war should spare the poor man's life, and send him to his long wished-for home, with the trifling loss of a leg, or an arm, he will at least have the consolation of reflecting that he might have lost them both; and should his starving family, in the bitterness of want, by chance reproach him for his incapacity to relieve them, he will no doubt silence their murmurs, and turn their sorrow into joy, by reminding them, that it was in the glorious cause of their king and country that they suffered. (p. 26)

Hucks's irony is perhaps a trifle heavy (though no more so than Johnson's in his essay on the Falkland Islands[1]), but the humanitarianism of his sentiment is both general enough to be acceptable and precise enough to be unmistakable as an attack on the war itself. In his preface he is tactful enough to make clear that the publication of his book at a time 'when the great scale of our political existence is in danger of sinking for ever' and 'rapine and oppression are desolating the fairest regions of Europe' may be considered as an 'intrusion'. He is equally tactful in the book itself. Moreover, while the tour was undertaken with Coleridge whose political and social views must have inflamed his own, the book was published under his own name and, since he was no longer under Coleridge's direct influence, his views had perhaps become more moderate. According to his second letter to Southey, Coleridge affirms that he had 'positively done nothing but dream of the System of no Property every step of the Way' (see p. 99 below) and in his letter to Henry Martin he states that he spent the tour 'now philosophizing with Hucks, now melancholizing by myself, or else indulging those day-dreams of Fancy, that make realities more gloomy' (see p. 99 below). We know from more precisely documented relationships between Coleridge and his friends just how demanding and compelling a friend Coleridge was. We cannot, therefore, believe that he was any less persuasive as Hucks's companion or that Hucks was not caught up in Coleridge's 'dream of the System of no Property'. Indeed, Coleridge talking seems to have been no less compelling than his own Ancient Mariner and asks for nothing better than an audience equally attentive, silent and passive.

Hucks's intimacy with Coleridge seemed to have ended with the completion of their tour and once they separated, it is likely that Hucks's conservatism reasserted itself. Certainly, by the time Hucks read Coleridge's dedicatory poem 'To the Rev. George Coleridge', included in his *Poems* of 1797, he was obviously disturbed enough by the possibility that Coleridge now considered him one of his false friends, to write his 'Lines Addressed to S. T. Coleridge' by way of self-defence. (See Appendix II). With a self-indulgence, even self-pity, which cannot be entirely overlooked, Coleridge had written of his friends:

> A brief while
> Some have preserv'd me from life's pelting ills;
> But, like a tree with leaves of feeble stem,

1. *The Yale Edition of the Works of Samuel Johnson*, ed. A. T. Hazen and J. H. Mitzendorf, 9 vols, New Haven, 1958–71, X. *Political Writings*, ed. Donald J. Greene, 1971, pp.346–86.

> If the clouds lasted, and a sudden breeze
> Ruffled the boughs, they on my head at once
> Dropped the collected shower; and some most false,
> False and fair-foliag'd as the Manchineel,
> Have tempted me to slumber in their shade
> E'en mid the storm; then breathing subtlest damps,
> Mix'd their own venom with the rain from Heaven,
> That I woke poison'd! [lines 20–30]

Indeed, in considering these lines none of Coleridge's friends could be blamed for wondering whether Coleridge now thought of him as 'most false, False' or as merely weak and unreliable. In his poem Hucks vigorously and generously asserts the strong loyalty of his friendship but is clearly sufficiently upset by the thought that his feelings for Coleridge had been so shrilly brought into question. By that time, however, it is also clear that Hucks saw friendship as being based upon mutual feelings of respect and affection and not upon shared views. Particularly at this early stage of his intellectual development few if any could be expected to keep pace with the rapidity with which Coleridge changed his opinions and his moods. If Coleridge totally absorbed Hucks's attention for a period, as he seems to have done during the tour of Wales, and then completely baffled him by his subsequent behaviour, we can now recognize this as a typical pattern in Coleridge's relationships.

Moreover, while there is no doubt that Hucks shared Coleridge's enthusiasms in 1794, as Coleridge's own views changed so his attitude towards his own past experience altered. By the time he came to write *Biographia Literaria*, he had little faith in the innate wisdom of natural man or in the moral advantages accruing to those who grow up in rural societies:

> Whatever may be concluded on the other side, from the stronger local attachments and enterprising spirit of the Swiss, and other mountaineers, applies to a particular mode of pastoral life, under forms of property that permit and beget manners truly republican, not to rustic life in general, or to the absence of artificial cultivation. On the contrary the mountaineers, whose manners have been so often eulogized, are in general better educated and greater readers than men of equal rank elsewhere. But where this is not the case, as among the peasantry of North Wales, the ancient mountains, with all their terrors and all their glories, are pictures to the blind, and music to the deaf. (Ch. XVII).[1]

Here Coleridge entirely repudiates his original attitude towards the 'peasantry of North Wales' so clearly stated in 1794, in order, (it

1. Ed. cit., II. 32.

must in fairness be pointed out) to undermine his friend Words-worth's view, embodied in the 1800 Preface to *Lyrical Ballads*, which is in all essentials identical to that he himself had held six years earlier.

Despite all inconsistencies and his remark to William Godwin in September 1800 that 'of North Wales my recollections are faint'[1], Coleridge did gain something from his tour of North Wales. In composing *The Ancient Mariner*, for instance, he recalled climbing Penmaenmawr; Hucks describes the incident:

> We rashly took the resolution to venture up this stupendous mountain [Penmaenmawr] without a guide, and therefore unknowingly fixed upon the most difficult part to ascend, and consequently were continually impeded by a vast number of unexpected obstructions. At length we surmounted every danger and difficulty, and safely arrived at the top; but the fatigue we had undergone, and the excessive heat of the day, deprived us, in a great degree, of that pleasure we should otherwise have received from the prospect, and occasioned a torment-ing thirst that we were not able to gratify; for water was an article which we searched for in vain. Preparing, in the utmost despondency, to descend, we accidentally turned over a large flat stone that concealed a little spring, which, thus obstructed, became absorbed under the surface of the earth. The parched-up soldier of Alexander's army could not have felt greater joy in the discovery of his little treasure, than we did of ours. (pp. 30–1)

Many years later, Coleridge is recorded as saying:

> I took the thought of grinning for joy, in that poem ['The Ancient Mariner'], from my companion's remark to me, when we had climbed to the top of Plinlimmon [sic. Penmaenmawr is intended] and were nearly dead with thirst. We could not speak from the constriction, till we found a little puddle under a stone. He said to me, 'You grinned like an idiot!' He had done the same. (*Table Talk*, 31 May 1830)

In his letter to Henry Martin, Coleridge refers briefly to this experience; 'at the imminent hazard of our Lives [we] scaled the very Summit of Penmaenmawr—it was a most dreadful expedition' (p. 103 below). However, if the images of thirst in *The Ancient Mariner* originate from this experience, since Penmaenmawr overlooks the sea perhaps it also gave rise to other images in the poem such as

> Water, water, everywhere
> Ne any drop to drink.

We also know from his letters and the handful of poems he wrote during the tour—'Lines written at the King's Arms, Ross', 'On Bala

1. *Letters* I. 620.

Hill', 'The Faded Flower', 'To a Beautiful Spring in a Village', and 'Perspiration' (the first of them sent from Gloucester to Southey)—that Coleridge suffered throughout the tour from heat and thirst, both of which are so powerfully evoked in the later poem:

> With throats unslack'd, with black lips bak'd
> Agape they hear'd me call:
> Gramercy! they for joy did grin
> And all at once their breath drew in,
> As they were drinking all. (1798 text, lines 154–8)

Furthermore, having spent the night at Caernarfon, three of the travellers re-crossed the Menai Straits to Anglesey and returned in the rain as it began to grow dark:

> the water was much agitated, so that without the addition of the rain, which came down in torrents, the spray of the sea would have completely made us wet through; but, in the midst of our distress, we were agreeably interested by a sight as beautiful to us as it was novel; the surface of the water suddenly assumed a luminous appearance, now and then relapsing into an impenetrable gloom, and then again re-lumined, it conveyed to the mind some idea of what the poets describe of Phlegethon in the shades below. (p. 43)

Classical Phlegethon, the river of fire that runs through Hades, is probably not the source of the image of the luminous colours of the water-snakes. On the other hand, the experience described by Hucks of intermittent colours flashing on the waters of the Menai Straits, whether experienced directly by Coleridge (as is probable) or reported vividly to him by his companions, is certainly a possible source of the image at the turning-point of the whole poem:

> Blue, glossy green, and velvet black
> They coil'd and swam; and every track
> Was a flash of golden fire (1798 text, lines 271–3)

Also the abrupt change from agitated distress arrested by the beauty of the luminous fire on the water is consistent with the sudden change of tone and feeling at this critical point in the poem.

There can be no doubt that, whatever Coleridge's particular debts to the incidents on his tour of North Wales, the memory of it persisted. If it provided nothing more, the tour created common ground between him and Wordsworth long before they met in 1797, and this alone is sufficient to lend Hucks's book significance. However, although it is most unlikely that the travellers recognized the fact, they were indebted to Wordsworth from the beginning. In his opening pages Hucks makes clear just how novel an idea a walking tour really was in 1794:

lxv

The mode of travelling which we have adopted, at the first view promises nothing remarkably alluring; and I think you were of opinion that our resolution was not equal to the undertaking of such an enterprise, and treated the whole plan as visionary and romantic. (pp. 4–5)

Walking for pleasure was, Hucks assumes, something of a new idea. Pilgrims walked to shrines and the peasantry walked because they could afford no easier form of transport, but only recently had Cambridge undergraduates walked thus, combining exercise in the open air with the pleasure of touring. Even Coleridge identified with the peasants in his poem 'Perspiration, A Travelling Eclogue', or, at least, he implied that only aristocrats would ride in coaches:

> The Dust flies smothering, as on clatt'ring Wheels
> Loath'd Aristocracy careers along.   (lines 1–2)

Moreover, in his poem 'On Bala Hill' he makes clear that walking really is exhausting exercise:

> With many a weary step at length I gain
> Thy summit, Bala! . . . 'Twas a long way and tedious.

Nonetheless, by the end of the tour Hucks was able to say that they were in good health and that in spite of 'wholesome fatigue' and all its inconveniences, he would not have travelled other than on foot. He bravely concludes:

> I do not hesitate a moment to say, that were I to make the same tour again, or one through a similar country, I should certainly perform it on foot, both from motives of convenience and independency. (pp. 58–9)

By Hucks's reckoning, he had travelled 629 miles from Cambridge to Bristol in just over two months. Yet Wordsworth, always an original, had pioneered the pedestrian tour on a scale that makes Hucks and his companion's efforts seem rather feeble. In 1790 Wordsworth and his Welsh friend Robert Jones undertook a complete 'grand tour' on foot and between July and October walked from London through France to Switzerland and the Alps and back again. As Mary Moorman says, 'Wordsworth and Jones may be regarded as the pioneers of the great company who, from their day to the hikers and ramblers of our own, have claimed to walk for pleasure over hill and dale'.[1] Whether Hucks and Coleridge would ever have contemplated a walk of this kind we do not know but the fact of the war with France put a continental tour out of the question. Indeed, it was doubtless because the Continent was closed

1. *William Wordsworth. A Biography. The Early Years 1770–1803*, 1968 edn., p. 131.

to tourists that they turned their attentions to another region of Great Britain and it is from this period that Wales became a tourist attraction.

Here, too, Coleridge had been anticipated by Wordsworth. In 1791 Wordsworth spent nearly four months with Robert Jones's family at Plas-yn-Llan, not far from Ruthin. In the dedicatory letter addressed to Robert Jones that he prefixed to his poem *Descriptive Sketches*, Wordsworth makes clear that he and Robert Jones walked over much of the route taken by Coleridge three years later:

> . . . I might have inscribed to you a description of some of the features of your native mountains, through which we have wandered together, in the same manner [as through the Alps], with so much pleasure. But the sea-sunsets, which give such splendour to the Vale of Clwyd, Snowdon, the chair of Idris, the quiet village of Bethgelert, Menai and the Druids, the Alpine steeps of the Conway, and the still more interesting windings of the wizard stream of the Dee, remain yet untouched.

Wordsworth visited Robert Jones's home again in 1793, this time walking to the Wye Valley and visiting Tintern for the first time (Coleridge did not accompany Hucks to Tintern in 1794) before reaching North Wales by way of Hay-on-Wye and Builth Wells. Wordsworth drew heavily on his experiences in Wales in his poetry, not only in *Tintern Abbey* and in the climactic vision of *The Prelude* where he describes the 1791 ascent of Snowdon, but in many other poems. There can be no doubt that during their great period of friendship which established Romantic poetry as the predominant mode, both Wordsworth and Coleridge shared, among other things, their memories of the striking and unique beauty of Wales. Hucks's book, therefore, deserves a secure place not only among travel journals but also as part of the literature of the Romantic Movement.

Sketch-Map of the Route.

A
PEDESTRIAN TOUR

THROUGH

NORTH WALES,

IN A

SERIES OF LETTERS.

By J. HUCKS, B.A.

With gold and gems if Chilian mountains glow,
If bleak and barren Cambria's hills arise,
There plague and poison, lust and rapine grow,
Here peaceful are the vales, and pure the skies,
And freedom fires the soul, and sparkles in the eyes.
THE MINSTREL.

London:

Printed for J. DEBRETT, Piccadilly; and J.
EDWARDS, Pall Mall.

Sold also by W. H. LUNN, B. FLOWER, and J. DEIGHTON,
Cambridge; Messrs. BINNS, and GREENWOOD, Leeds;
and Messrs. DYER, and TREWMAN, Exeter.

1795.

Preface

AT a time so peculiarly alarming to the affairs of this country, that every hour comes attended with some fresh calamity: when reason and justice are suffering in the conflict of nations: when rapine and oppression are desolating the fairest regions of Europe: in short, when the common interests of humanity, when every dear and invaluable privilege, that can render society lovely and desirable, is altogether neglected or forgotten, and the happy re-union of liberty and tranquillity, more the object of our wishes than our expectations; in such an eventful, but fatal, period of the political drama, the following letters may probably be considered as an intrusion upon the public attention, too much absorbed in the nice intrigues of the cabinet and the field, to unbend their thoughts to lighter pursuits, when the great scale of our political existence is in danger of sinking for ever.

Lest any such argument should be adduced against him, the author begs leave to make one observation, (viz.) That he has written neither for the statesman, the general, or the politician; he is sensible, that from the nature of the subject, his little work will not be extended amongst a very large class of readers; the amusement of an individual was originally the sole object of the following letters, but he has ventured to make them public, under the hope that they may, in some measure, contribute to the satisfaction of those who have not seen, yet may wish to become familiar with, the outlines of a country, so dissimilar in every respect to England; and to whom a slight sketch of the most prominent

2

features of its inhabitants, may not appear either tedious or uninteresting; and he flatters himself, they will not be unacceptable to those, who, like himself, might be induced to explore the beautiful scenery of North Wales; and to whom the short, though probably imperfect account of it there given, may prove an useful companion, to direct them in their progress through a country, to which they might be altogether unacquainted.

He claims the indulgence of his readers for the tautology and egotism, almost inseparable from works of such a description; but he has, as much as possible, endeavoured to avoid a repetition of names, and for this reason, has, in most cases, spoken of himself as being the only spectator; at the same time, in justice to those who accompanied him, he takes this opportunity of acknowledging himself, upon many occasions, greatly indebted to them for many interesting remarks and useful information, which otherwise he could not have had the means of acquiring.

Since he first conceived the design of publishing these letters, some necessary additions have been made, and a short Appendix added, for the sake of giving them a more connected form; for there were a few places, which owing to particular circumstances, it was not in his power to see, and a short account of these, together with some other detached observations, compose the Appendix, to which also are subjoined the names of the most noted places that they visited in the course of their route, and their distances from each other. Those marked with one or more asterisks, imply the number of nights they remained at each.

A Pedestrian Tour, &c. &c. &c.

LETTER I.

BALA, North Wales, July 11, 1794.

SURROUNDED on all sides by cloud-capt mountains; arrived amongst a people, to whose language I am a perfect stranger, and whose manners and customs are as eccentric as they are singular, every circumstance attracts attention, and every object excites admiration. But it is with pleasure, my dear friend, that I cease for a while from contemplating the scene around me, and turn to that which I have so lately quitted: memory willingly lingers round a spot where the mind has not been much oppressed with sorrow or care; and I must, in justice, acknowledge, that during a residence of three years at Cambridge, the happiness I there enjoyed was scarcely ever interrupted, or overshadowed even by the smallest cloud of misfortune; a retrospect will therefore prove to me a constant source of satisfaction, because the memory of the past will not be accompanied with images of regret, or any other cause of sorrow or reproach. It will be peculiarly pleasing to me to write to you from time to time, and give you some account of our 'Travels' History,' to relate to you all our 'most disastrous chances and moving accidents by flood or field;' for in every thing which concerned us, you were pleased to express yourself particularly interested, and I assure you, it is not alone in compliance with your earnest and repeated request, but under the immediate impulse of my own wishes and inclination, that I am now induced to write to you.

The mode of travelling which we have adopted,

at the first view promises nothing remarkably alluring; and I think you were of opinion that our resolution was not equal to the undertaking of such an enterprise, and treated the whole plan as visionary and romantic. But I flatter myself you will now be convinced we are in earnest, especially when I tell you that experience has more than ever confirmed us in our original intention; for the pleasure we have hitherto derived from our progress, has much exceeded our most sanguine expectations.

I shall now proceed to give you a short detail of occurrences, from the day on which my compagnon de voyage and myself departed from Cambridge, to the present time. Behold us, then, more like two pilgrims performing a journey to the tomb of some wonder-working saint, than men travelling for their pleasure and amusement. We are so completely metamorphosed, that I much doubt whether you would recognise us through our disguise; we carry our clothes, &c. in a wallet or knapsack, from which we have not hitherto experienced the slightest inconvenience: as for all ideas of appearance and gentility, they are entirely out of the question—our object is to see, not to be seen; and if I thought I had one acquaintance who would be ashamed of me and my knapsack, seated by the fire side of an honest Welsh peasant, in a country village, I should not only make myself perfectly easy on my own account, but should be induced to pity and despise him for his weakness.

We made some stay at Oxford, where we experienced the utmost hospitality and attention; and then prosecuted our route by way of Gloucester, Ross, Hereford, Bishop's Castle, &c. I have annexed the names of the places we have passed through in their regular order, as well as their distances from each other, so that you will perceive we have not fatigued ourselves with very long marches.

5

It is not my intention to trouble you with a minute description of places; or with uninteresting accounts of individuals, from which you would not derive any very desirable information in the perusal, nor I any gratification in the relation. The feelings of men generally harmonize with their situation; and sublime images must naturally arise in the mind, when the external objects of its contemplation are accompanied with any thing peculiarly grand or majestic: under such impressions I cannot, when I am upon the summit of a mountain, with a beautiful and fertile country widely extending upon the sight, think of any thing but the prospect before me; nor in admiring a cathedral constructed with all the elegance of finished architecture, could I reduce my thoughts to the rule and compass in order to measure its height and dimensions, or enter into a critique upon the justness of its proportions; the form would triumph over the matter, and drive every other consideration to a distance: and after contemplating the venerable remains of some once celebrated fabric, I could not patiently endure to give an historical detail of its founder, the different benefactors to whom it has been indebted, or the charters and privileges it has enjoyed. But they are not alone sublime situations which excite sublime ideas; every object in nature is interesting, and wherever nature is, I feel similar sensations; mountains and valleys, rivers and rivulets, nay the smallest plants that are trodden under our feet, unseen or unregarded, are inexhaustible sources, to a contemplative mind, of gratification and delight.

> O how can'st thou renounce the boundless store
> Of charms, which nature to her vot'ry yields!
> The warbling woodland, the resounding shore,
> The pomp of groves, and garniture of fields;
> All that the genial ray of morning gilds,
> And all that echoes to the song of even;
> All that the mountain's sheltering bosom shields,

6

And all the dread magnificence of heaven;
O how can'st thou renounce, and hope to be
forgiven!

The Minstrel.

Let the atheist or the *manicheist* (if such there are in
reality, as I know there are some professedly), pay a
little attention to the philosophy of nature, ever
changing, but still connected, at once majestic but
simple, disdaining the rules and frigid boundaries
of art, at the same time modelled upon the most
beautiful and graceful proportion—their short-lived
doubts must instantly vanish, and their daring
incredulity yield to the most rational and forcible
conviction; they must then confess that this world
could never have been created by chance, or be the
work of a *malignant* deity; but that it bears the
traces of a hand divine, the beautiful production of
a benevolent, eternal, and intellectual being. I can
scarcely believe there is that man existing, who can
see without emotion the beauteous orb of day rising
in the east, and in the evening behold its setting
beams; who can look with apathy upon the moon
when she gilds the brow of night, and all the
numerous host of stars, the panoply of heaven, that
shine around her; who equally unmoved by storms
and sunshine, by calms and tempests, can yet be
induced, from a pitiful and weak despair of a happy
futurity, from a wilful incredulity, or a misguided
scepticism, to deny the great and generating cause
of all effects! The chief object of this expedition,
and from which I hope to derive the greatest
pleasure, is to explore the hidden beauties of nature
unmechanized by the ingenuity of man; as well as to
make some observations upon the human character
under every different attitude it may assume; in
short, to study nature in her works, and man in
society. The lower orders of people in this part of
Great Britain have as yet presented to me only a
picture of humiliation and wretchedness. Whether
this be the general character, or but a partial

7

appearance of the country, I shall have other opportunities of discovering in the prosecution of my journey: at present I am far from entertaining a favourable opinion of their stock of happiness; undeniably there are numerous examples of apparent cheerfulness and content to be found amongst the poor inhabitants of a mud-built cottage; but are not the social endearments of domestic life (the only source of enjoyment amongst the lower order of mankind), too often imbittered by repeated difficulties and distresses, and rendered so many aggravating circumstances to the wounded recollection of a parent, surrounded by a numerous and helpless family who look up to him for protection and support, which he is utterly unable to afford them? I believe and hope that such instances of want and degradation are rare; but very few of them are requisite to convince any man, capable of feeling for others as he would for himself, that the aggregate of happiness, amongst the lower species of our fellow-creatures, does not bear a just proportion to that of pain, and that their condition is capable of very essential improvement. Under the pressure of poverty and misfortune, the mind oftentimes forgets its noble nature, and the proper degree of estimation with which it should regard its own existence: and this is the case with that description of men here spoken of. To remove then this evil, by doing away the cause of the complaint (viz. Oppression), would be a work well worthy the attention of every friend of mankind. Under whatever circumstances of poverty and inferiority many of our fellow-creatures may be placed, yet they have a just claim upon our protection and support; for though habit, and the hard hand of oppressive want, may have contracted the modes of thinking amongst them, yet they undoubtedly possess intellects, which, if properly cultivated, might equally adorn a senate, or a forum, with those who are called their superiors, from the mere accidental circumstances

8

of wealth, or hereditary distinctions. A human being, as he comes originally from the hand of nature, is every where the same; the capacity of improvement, the talents and virtues which the mind is capable of acquiring and exercising, are to every state of society alike inherent. Surely then all must rejoice in the melioration of that state, since to contribute to its improvement is the noblest pursuit of individuals, and ought to be the sole end of all governments; but the sacred principles of the social compact are no longer regarded, and that which should be the first is now become the last care or consideration of legislative science. To say that the state of society cannot be improved, is either to assert its perfection, to confess that all exertions to improve that state would be vain, or that these political evils are either necessary or irremediable. To the first of these arguments, if they can be deemed worthy of such a denomination, there is no necessity to reply, because it carries with it its own conviction; and with respect to the last, no one will hesitate to pronounce it an impious reflection upon the benevolence of the Creator, whose intention could never be to subject man to any species of political tyranny whatever; and well indeed might this fair creation and celestial harmony be called a Manichean system, or work of a malevolent being, if he could sanction upon this globe the detestable crimes, and abhorred impieties committed under the patronage, and often the immediate consequence, of vicious and corrupted governments; or if he could fix so narrow and confined a boundary to human happiness.

The face of the country, as far as this place, is for the most part dull and uninteresting, our road lying chiefly over long and barren mountains, which is pretty much the general appearance of the interior part of North Wales, of which Bala is nearly the center; few living creatures cheer these dreary

9

scenes, but here and there a miserable hut, that ill conceals its wretched inhabitants, and a few poor sheep, thinly scattered over the steep sides of the mountain, or picking the short grass from the almost naked summit of the shaggy rock; we congratulate ourselves, therefore, on our present situation, and on having left behind us the worst part of our tour; but there are some places which must be excepted from this general censure, and these I shall briefly take notice of. We slept at the King's Arms at Ross, which was formerly the habitation of that celebrated character who usually goes by the name of the 'Man of Ross'. He was truly a friend to the human kind.—He gave his worldly goods, as far as they would go, to the unfortunate; and his best wishes and unqualified compassion to all; his memory is still revered, and his loss still lamented. I cannot omit sending you a few lines which my fellow traveller scribbled upon a window shutter, unlike the general style of composition which such places abound with:

'Richer than misers o'er their countless hoards,
Nobler than kings or king-polluted lords;
Here dwelt the Man of Ross. O traveller hear,
Departed merit claims the rev'rend tear;
Friend to the friendless, to the sick man health,
With generous joy he viewed his modest wealth;
He heard the widow's heav'n-breath'd prayer of praise,
He markd the shelter'd orphan's tearful gaze;
And o'er the dowried virgins snowy cheek,
Bade bridal love suffuse its blushes meek.
If'neath this roof thy wine cheer'd moments pass,
Fill to the good man's name one grateful glass,
To higher zest shall mem'ry wake thy soul,
And virtue mingle in the ennobled bowl.
But if like me thro' life's distressful scene,
Lonely and sad thy pilgrimage hath been,
And if thy breast with heart-sick anguish fraught,
Thou journeyest onward tempest-tost in thought,

Here cheat thy cares—in generous visions melt,
And dream of goodness thou hast never felt.'

Montgomery is a neat town, and pleasantly situated; but except St. Asaph, it is one of the smallest capital towns in the king's dominions. In the neighbourhood of Welsh Pool, upon a most beautiful eminence, stands Powis castle, formerly called Pool castle, from its vicinity to Welsh Pool; it was built A.D. 1110, by Cadogan ap Bledhyn, who was not long suffered to enjoy it, before he was murdered by his nephew Madoc. Such horrid crimes, however, were so familiar to those days, and so little regarded, that they were frequently committed with impunity, and the offenders might always escape by a fine or dispensation. The castle commands an extensive view of a fertile vale, through which the Severn, yet in its infancy, rolls gently along. The road from thence to Llanvilling is very intricate, and we contrived to lose our way more than once, notwithstanding we had been told it was as straight as an arrow; we wanted about five miles of the latter place, when we met with an honest Cambrian of a very respectable appearance—we did not fail to make some enquiry of him concerning our road; he stopped his horse very politely, and informed us that he was then returning from Llanvilling, the place of his nativity, which he had not seen for more than twenty years before; he added that we should find an excellent inn, and plenty of the best ale in Wales; he then wished us a pleasant walk, assuring us we should meet with princely accommodations, and earnestly recommending the sign of the *goat*, at the same time advising us to make use of his name, for Owen ap Jones ap Evans was as well known as any name in Wales. I relate this little anecdote to you, because I think the character of a people is best delineated by their actions, and their leading features are as completely developed by an action, or an anecdote of themselves, apparently insignificant, as they could possibly be in five hundred

11

philosophical pages upon the nature of climate, situation, or government, and the physical causes and effects they may have upon the human genius and disposition. We were much diverted with the whole of our walk to Llanvilling, particularly with the small but pleasant river Verniew, which we crossed. It was late when we arrived, and were much disappointed with respect to those excellent accommodations our honest friend had hinted at, for we could get nothing but dry bread and bad cheese, poor cheer for two hungry travellers that had scarcely eat any thing since breakfast.

Llangunnog is singularly situated, surrounded on all sides by barren and sandy hills. The place consists only of a few houses, amongst which there is a small building ycleped a church, where once a week a sermon is delivered in the Welsh language. Whilst we were at dinner in a little ale-house (which by the bye was the only one in the place), we had a glance at the clergyman, who happened to enter the house at that very time; his appearance altogether bespoke an inferiority of condition, disgraceful to that respectable body of which he was a member; upon observing us, he abruptly went out, while our landlady informed us, with an air of triumph, as if he was something superior to the rest of mankind, that 'that was the parson.' He was standing near the house when we went out, and wishing to enter into conversation with him, I desired him to inform me which was the direct road to Bala; he appeared somewhat confused, and waving his hand towards the way we had enquired for, answered only by the monosyllable 'that,' and walked hastily away. I felt much hurt, and at the same time a great degree of admiration, both at his truly laconic answer, as well as at his manner of address, in which pride seemed to be struggling with poverty; in such a situation any degree of sensibility would be to him rather a misfortune than a blessing. Fixed to a spot in which there could be no one proper for his company, or capable of his conversation, he might be driven to pass his evenings, for the sake of society, with people very far inferior to him, and by degrees lose those finer qualities of the mind, that refinement of action as well as of thought, which properly distinguish the gentleman from the honest but blunt peasant, or the industrious mechanic. I should not have mentioned this circumstance, but that it bears some credible testimony to the common report of the shameful and scanty provision made for the Welsh clergy; which by no means enables them to assume that character so essentially necessary to the ministers of christianity. I do not wish to insinuate that there is any disgrace in poverty, but certainly the ignorant and uninstructed too frequently treat their teachers with a respect proportioned to their appearance; and if this be true, it calls loudly for laws and regulations which shall be more favourable to the lower clergy in general. The act of parliament confines the salaries of curates within twelve and fifty pounds per annum, whereas it ought to have been proportioned either to the duty performed, or the value of the benefice itself. Let us take one instance—a curate serves two churches ten miles distant from each other; whilst the incumbent, or vicar, who holds them both, and receives for the joint value of the tithes, five hundred pounds per annum, allows his curate, who does all the duty, only forty pounds per annum. This cannot be considered as an adequate compensation, even for the labour; and adding the respectability and appearance of the profession, it is indeed contemptible and insignificant.*

*The following extract is a singular confirmation of the above statement.

'The curates of the undernamed places, were lately elected by the trustees of Mr. Stock's liberal donation, to receive ten pounds each, viz.

The curate of Llanswrog, in Anglesea, 5 young children, and 25l. per annum.

13

Bala is situated upon the borders of a large lake, eleven miles in circumference, and four and a half long. It abounds with pike, perch, trout, and other fish; the country around is grand and sublime, but not interesting; stupendous mountains seem 'to mix their heads with dropping clouds,' but with respect to cultivation, or even verdure, they are entirely destitute; every necessary article of life is here more than commonly reasonable; fifty pound at Bala would go as far as an hundred in most parts of England. We were yesterday much diverted with a curious political conversation carried on at the inn, in the room which we in part occupied, at a table by ourselves; at another, were seated the clergyman, the exciseman, the attorney, the apothecary, and I suppose, by his appearance, the barber of the place, &c. these were met upon business over a bowl of punch, which seemed to constitute the chief part of it; whilst in an opposite corner of the room, two more decent looking people were enjoying themselves in a similar manner. The clergyman gave aloud 'Church and King,' as a toast, and soon after one of our neighbours at the other table, proposed 'General Washington' to his friend; this created a

Ditto of Beguiley and Bettus, Radnorshire, 9 young children, 35l. per annum.

Ditto of Michaelstone Vedow, Monmouthshire, 8 young children, 25l. per annum.

Ditto of Langadfan, Montgomeryshire, 5 young children, 25l. per annum.

Ditto of Ireby, in Cumberland, 8 young children, 25l. per annum.

Ditto of Llanvair, Monmouthshire, 4 young children, 13l. per annum.

Ditto of Burwarton and Wheathill, Shropshire, 7 young children, 30l. per annum.

Ditto of Abernorlish, Caermarthenshire, 8 young children, 18l. per annum.

The curate of Sebergham, Cumberland, 8 young children, 30l. per annum.

The curate of Silian, Cardiganshire, 6 young children, 15l. per annum.

This valuable charity is annually given to ten poor curates who have large families; and reflects the highest honour on the worthy donor.'

14

great commotion amongst the large party; for the clergyman immediately standing up gave as his second toast 'may all *Demicrats* be *gullotin'd*,' when the other filling *his* glass, added, 'may all fools be gullotin'd, and then I knows who'll be the first'; after this ensued a violent and dreadful battle of tongues, in which these people excel in an extraordinary degree. The clergyman defended his toast, on the grounds that it shewed his zeal in a good cause, forgetting that it was necessary first to prove the merit of the sentiment, as united by him, and after that, to shew that his zeal was best made known as a clergyman, by his benevolent and truly pious wish. But majors and minors were things which this zealous and humane defender of his church and king had little regard for. The clamour at length became so loud, that we soon withdrew ourselves from the scene of contention, and left the combatants to settle the point in the best manner they could; though it seemed to me that it required more sophistry than the clergyman had displayed, and more wit than the other possessed, to justify or even excuse themselves. From hence the traveller may easily visit the two Arrans, *viz.* Arran Mowddwy, and Arran Penllyn, both of them of a stupendous size, but inferior to Snowdon, Cader Idris, or Paenmanmawr. We intend to proceed to-morrow as far as Langollen; but I will not defer closing a letter which I have imperceptibly lengthened far beyond my original design; and believe me, my dear friend, that I subscribe myself with sincerity,

Your's affectionately, &c.

I.H.

LETTER II.

DENBIGH, July 14, 1794.

IT was late in the evening when we left Bala, and

therefore, contrary to our original intentions, we took up our quarters for the night, at the Druid house, a solitary place only eight miles distant from that which we had last quitted; and early the following morning we pursued our journey to Llangollen. The face of the country now became more interesting. The scene gradually assumed a less rugged appearance; the dark brown mountain, and the desolated heath, softened by distance, formed a beautiful contrast to the wild and irregular scenery that succeeded. We felt our spirits, which had before been depressed from the barren and gloomy country we had traversed, now much exhilarated, and we seemed to breathe a freer air. There is an analogy in nature throughout, from the most torpid state of vegetable existence to the most refined subtlety of animal life; and he who has not considered this attentively, will be surprised, upon reflection, to perceive that his own self importance is solely derived from the contemplation of external objects; for deprive him of these, shut him out from nature, suppose him to be totally unacquainted with the harmony of this beautiful sphere, he must consider himself in the most contemptible point of view, created for no purpose, endued with powers of perception and reasoning for no possible good; his would be a mere comfortless state of existence, with a mind that could have no adequate idea, if any at all, of the deity; his would be a situation unworthy the character of his species, and little elevated above the brute creation. Certainly there is a chain of causes and effects throughout every creative world, whether mineral, vegetable, or animal; and all has an effect upon the mind of man. When we approach a desolate and cloud-capt country, an uncultivated and dreary scene, what is the cause that we frequently feel a damp upon our spirits? Why does it affect the mind, as it were, with a leaden weight, and depress the active springs of the imagination? It is from the analogy which

16

nature, under every form she may assume, bears to the varied life of man. Memory backward turns her view, and assimilates the objects before her, to some certain passage of our life, that impresses upon the mind a shade of melancholy or joy, according as those passages may have been marked with pleasure, or with pain. It is not therefore that there is any absolute impression made upon the mind, from the scene before us, whether it be bright with sunshine, or overcast with clouds, but it is memory which associates to it some event, or transaction of former years, which, though scarcely perceptible, is the cause of such an effect. Our road wound along the banks of the river Dee, which falls murmuring over its pebbled bed at the foot of the mountains, whose steep sides are covered with wood of the largest growth, here and there the shaggy rock, more than half concealed by the surrounding foliage, peering its broken summit beyond the most extended branches, and threatening, by its fall, to obstruct the course of the river beneath; whilst the spreading beach-tree, and mountain ash, that are found in great abundance upon its banks, dipping their slender branches in the stream, and above all, upon the lofty summit of a conical mountain, the castle Dinas Brân, rising in ruined majesty; at once afford an interesting spectacle of grandeur and sublimity, as well as of beauty and cultivation. Llangollen is most delightfully situated, but the place itself has nothing to boast of, except a very good inn which fortunately belies its appearance. We were entertained, upon our arrival, by a celebrated Welsh harper, who tuned his strings to so Orphean a measure, that a crowd soon collected round the door of our little inn, some of whom began to dance after the rustic fashion of their country; the simplicity of former times struck forcibly upon my mind, and brought back the pleasing recollection of those happy ages, when riches and luxury had not corrupted the heart of man; but when all mankind

17

were brothers, and the interest of one became the interest of all. It afforded me a satisfaction I had never before experienced, to find myself amongst a people, who act with all the simplicity of nature; totally destitute of the assumed appearance, and artificial manners of more modern times. The Welsh musick assimilates to the genius of the people, and is in general wild and irregular, but often plaintive, and always affecting; for the harp is perhaps more calculated to express the extremes of passion than any other instrument; it is astonishing with what skill and execution it is sometimes played upon, and with what enthusiasm the country people listen to it; insomuch that I have no doubt the fine tones of a Cramer, or a Clementi, would be totally disregarded by these honest people, for the humble strains of a blind Welsh harper. The musical amateur of the present day would despise so vulgar a taste; for with him the Italian school is alone supportable; I dare not therefore profess myself an admirer of simple and unaffected musick, or, in other words, prefer that which penetrates to the heart, to that which goes no farther than the ear; because I should be immediately condemned as a Goth, Vandal, or barbarian. I shall venture however to observe, that it appears to me there can be no absolute criterion of musick; that being the best, which touches the passions, and affects the feelings in the greatest degree, by any assemblage of sounds whatsoever; and if this be true, a Welsh harp, or an Irish bagpipe (risum teneatis amici) well executed, is infinitely superior to all the fiddle strings and kettle drums of Italy or Venice.

There are two roads from Llangollen to Wrexham, one on each side of the River Dee; the best is that on the right, which we took; but it is rather the longest. This road is carried upon the high grounds, from whence the prospect is delightful. The river, winding through the valleys, sometimes intercepted

18

by a rising ground or thick wood, then opening full upon the view, the luxuriance of nature is richly displayed through the whole landscape. Upon the hill above us were seen the dark figures of the miners; the confused noise of the men, who were preparing to descend these gloomy caverns, and of the busy team, returning with its ponderous load; while the thick volumes of black smoke, that continued to ascend into a clear and beautiful atmosphere, formed an uncommon and striking contrast. On the other side, the river, stealing through the valley, had, by its overflowing, contributed to give it the richest appearance of fertility; in some places the mower, almost buried under the high grass, often paused from his labour; in others, the sharp sound of the grinding stone, the loud laugh, or toil-subduing song, were frequently heard: on the sides of the opposite hills were scattered the modest hamlets that owned these industrious peasants; behind us, at some distance, the whitened spire, and part of the little town we had left, were still visible; whilst over all, the setting sun cast its softened tints, a part of the valley only being shaded by the interposition of a neighbouring mountain, whose summit still retained in glowing colours the last rays of the departing day. On the right, a little farther on, there is a fine view of Chirk castle, and on the left, of Winstay; the first, the seat of Mr. Middleton, the last of Sir Watkin William Wynne. About half way from Llangollen to Wrexham, we crossed a bridge where the two roads meet, and then we bad adieu to the River Dee, which kept its course afterwards to the right of us. Wrexham is a large populous and well built town; there is a very elegant tower belonging to the church, reputed to be a great curiosity. But I have very little pleasure in viewing the works of art; and indeed, human ingenuity of any kind or description, excites rather my admiration than my love: as far as they have contributed to soften the manners of mankind, it is

19

well; but have they not also tended to corrupt and deprave them? If, on the one hand, they have contributed to their wants and conveniences; on the other, they have encouraged the excess, and afforded an unbounded gratification to the sensual passions; the fine arts, like so many handmaids, should ever be ready to attend, but not to command; to soften manners, but not to render them luxurious.—From Wrexham our road became less interesting; and for ten or twelve miles, presented nothing to recompence the fatigue of a long and tedious walk, until we had ascended a very high hill, when the vale of Clwyd, in all its beauty, unfolded upon the sight: it appeared like a moving picture, upon which nature had been prodigal of its colours. Hamlets, villages, towns, and castles, rose like enchantment upon this rich carpet, that seemed covered with wood and enclosures; in the midst of it, at the distance of about five miles, the town of Ruthin, partially appeared from the bosom of a most beautiful grove of trees; the vale on each side being bounded by a chain of lofty mountains, and far off, on a bold and rugged promontory, stood Denbigh, with its strong fortress, the undisputed mistress of this extended scene. The great defect of the vale, is its want of water; the little river Clwyd, which winds through it, not being perceptible at any distance, and in dry seasons quite choaked up; though on the contrary, in wet and rainy weather, it soon overflows the whole country, swelled by the torrents from the surrounding hills.* The land in the vale lying low, and consequently swampy, is, upon a nearer examination, rather coarse. We dined at Ruthin, where there are some remains of a castle, and reached Denbigh yesterday evening. This town

* This delightful vale is of an oval shape, twenty-six miles in length, and about eight wide in the broadest part; it is wholly bounded with high hills, excepting towards the Irish sea, where it ends in a marsh at Rydland.

Gentleman's Tour through Wales, &c.

is well built, and the principal street which is on the slope of the hill, is broad and clean, but there are very indifferent accommodations to be met with. After tea we took a walk to view the castle, whose venerable walls, rising high above the town, command a magnificent view of the whole vale.

The situation of this castle is admirably described by Churchyard, who lived in the time of Queen Elizabeth, and wrote his travels through North Wales in familiar verse.

'This castle stands on top of rocke most hye,
A mightie cragge, as hard as flint or steele;
A massie mount, whose stones so deepe doth lye,
That no device may well the bottome feele.
The rocke descends beneath the auntient towne,
About the which a stately wall goes downe,
With buyldings great, and posternes to the same,
That goes thro' rocke to give it greater fame.'

It was built in the reign of Edward the First, and garrisoned, in the time of Charles the First, by the royalists; but was obliged to surrender to the parliament army, after a gallant and vigorous defence; the breaches in the walls are vast, and serve to shew the strength and thickness of their construction. The royal and unfortunate fugitive, Charles the First, after his retreat from Chester, took up his abode for one night in this castle. But it was destined that he should be the first sacrifice to freedom; and neither armies nor castles, walls nor cannon, could protect him from the hands of justice; or prevent an oppressed people from avenging upon him not only his own, but the fœdal despotism, and worse than papal tyranny, of five preceding reigns. Wretched must be that government, and the people that live under it, when it becomes necessary to restrain the encroachments of arbitrary power, at the point of the sword; or to exact obedience to the will of the sovereign from the cannon's mouth. Denbigh is more of a venerable,

21

than a magnificent ruin, and would, of itself, have amply repaid me for all the fatigue I had undergone; I would not willingly exaggerate the accounts of what I have seen, or endeavour to paint things otherwise, than as they really are; for I am sensible, that the reader too often acquires false ideas of places and things, from the pompous description of the traveller, who thinks himself obliged to relate something of the marvellous, in order that the world may not ridicule him, for crossing seas or traversing desarts, in search of what he might have easily seen at home; and yet it often happens, that scenes, though too highly coloured, may have had that appearance, to the eye of the spectator, at the time he describes them; and that what appears to him extremely beautiful to-day, may to-morrow strike the imagination in a very different manner; for much depends on the hour of observation, and the temper of mind we are in, to enjoy the objects before us. I cannot avoid relating a ludicrous circumstance, that took place, whilst I was amusing myself with wandering about the castle; and observing the effect of the scenery, through the huge breach, or broken arches, that looked over an almost perpendicular precipice, into the vale below. The moon was just rising in the horizon, when I perceived two gentlemen approach; they seemed to be expatiating upon the beauty of the scene, and in very earnest conversation with each other, one of them frequently repeating parts of Shakespear, which I could not distinctly hear, with a very theatrical tone and action. But I cannot express to you how much I was delighted, when, upon their nearer approach, I overheard the theatrical gentleman propose to his companion (as he had brought his flute in his pocket), to retire into a remoter part of the castle, and play some *soft airs*; God bless thee for the thought, said I to myself, amidst these solitary ruins, by the faint light of the moon, to listen to the soft cadence of distant musick, stealing its mournful melody, on the deluded ear like 'sounds of heavenly harmony,' must be altogether a soothing and romantic occupation for the mind, accompanied with those pleasing sentiments of melancholy, that are better felt than described. Having chosen a convenient situation, and prepared myself for the supreme pleasure I was about to receive, lo! this romantic disciple of Orpheus, *struck up* the tender air of *Corporal Casey*. I quitted the castle in an agony of disappointment, and left these romantic gentlemen to enjoy their *soothing concert*, and solitary situation, undisturbed. I returned, however, soon after, and found to my great satisfaction that the coast was clear: nothing could be more awfully grand, than the scene before me, which I surveyed with a degree of admiration, not totally destitute of a superstitious fear. The venerable appearance of the whole fabric; walls, and battlements, rising in ruined majesty; broken arches, half covered by the creeping ivy, and enchanters nightshade, high gothic windows, which but displayed the horrible gloom that reigned within; the mouldering tower, shook by every storm, affording an asylum to the owl, the bat, and the raven, lone tenants of these desolate mansions; whilst the moon bursting from a dark cloud, threw a partial gleam upon the pile, and served, by its feeble light, to discover the deep gloom of the remoter parts. At the same time, a fearful stillness every where prevailed, except that it was now and then interrupted by low solemn sounds of wind, that seemed to sigh amongst the distant turrets; the intermediate pauses impressing upon my mind a mixture of awe and veneration, which the surrounding scenery greatly contributed to encrease.

The post is going out, so that I have only time to transcribe the following lines upon Denbigh castle, with which I shall close this letter,—Adieu.

23

DENBIGH CASTLE.

Now sad, and slow, borne far on dusky wing,
Sails the still eve; night from her ebon throne
Slow rising, scatters wide her mystic spells
O'er the tir'd world; and from yon murky clouds
Gleams the pale moon, diffusing holy light
Through many a midnight isle and silent scene.
Much musing on life's changeful scene, I view,
Proud pile! thy tempest beaten towers, that rear
Their heads sublime, and to the angry storm
Bid bold defiance, though their aged brows
Bear visible the marks of stern decay;
While superstition, with a phrensied eye,
And wildering fear, that horrid forms surveys,
Affright the lonely wanderer from thy walls.
    Far hence thou busy world, nor here intrude
Thy sounds of uproar, arguing much of care
And impotent alarms; behold, fond man,
This feeble monument of mortal pride,
Where time and desolation reign supreme
With wildest havock—o'er the solemn scene
In silence pause, and mark this pictur'd truth;
That not alone the proudest works of man
Must perish; but as this tow'ring fabric,
That lifts its forehead to the storm, till time
And the wild winds shall sweep it from its base;
Pass but a few short hours—the dream of life
Is fled, and to the cold grave sinks man's faded
    form.

LETTER III.

ABBER, July 16, 1794.

THE last letter which I wrote to you, my dear friend, was dated from Denbigh. I now resume my pen from a spot far different indeed, but not by any means destitute of beauty. We quitted the above-mentioned place with great reluctance, and often looked back upon its venerable ruins, contrasting them in different situations, with the surrounding objects. Intervening hills had scarcely shut them from our view, before we entered upon a wide common, from whence a delightful prospect (terminated only by the sea), lay extended before the eye; on the edge of the common ran the rapid river Elwy, which we crossed, over a very beautiful bridge, with one noble arch.—The view of the river with its rocky shore, excavated in the most romantic manner—and the simple cottage embosomed within the dark wood that rose above it, formed an interesting perspective section through the arch of this bridge.

St. Asaph is a small neat town, situated upon the declivity of a hill, at the foot of which runs the river Clwyd. About three miles on this side of Holywell, there is a very extensive prospect. From the summit of a hill, we commanded a view of the Dee, incorporating its waters with the ocean. Far beyond, though considerably involved in a thick smoke, appeared Liverpool, the seat of busy commerce; and to the right, Park-gate, a favourite watering place, the abode of pleasure, and of song. I could not help smiling at the present appearance of the river Dee, compared with what it was when I formerly beheld it; at that time unconscious of its future greatness, it murmured over its craggy bed, or smoothly glided through the meadows and rich pastures, where numerous herds of cattle were feeding, or seeking to allay the sultry heat, in the midst of the stream. Many humble cottages rose upon its banks, presenting interesting pictures of content and happiness; children busily employed in picking sloes from the bushes that hung over the stream, or amusing themselves with throwing pebbles into the water, thus sporting with time, and 'reckless that age and sorrow with icy hand hung over them.' In another place a rough alpine bridge, thrown across the river, afforded a precarious passage to the cottager, in haste to reach his simple home, and share with his little family the produce of his daily toil.—Far different did it now strike the eye:—a noble river pouring its mighty waters into the bosom of the ocean; towns and cities rising upon its shores, big with the vanities of man, and fleets of merchantmen proudly floating in with the tide, laden with the wealth of the world.

Holywell is a clean built town, surrounded by a most beautiful country. There is a manufacture established at this place, that once gave bread to thousands, but alas! the loom is now forsaken for the sword, and the busy roof of industry exchanged for the sickly tent.

The town and neighbourhood, as might be expected, abound with numbers of poor women and children, who are half starving, whilst their husbands, fathers, and brothers, are gloriously signalizing themselves in the service of their country; and if by chance the ruthless sword of war should spare the poor man's life, and send him to his long wished-for home, with the trifling loss of a leg, or an arm, he will at least have the consolation of reflecting that he might have lost them both; and should his starving family, in the bitterness of want, by chance reproach him for his incapacity to relieve them, he will no doubt silence their murmurs, and turn their sorrow into joy, by reminding them, that it was in the glorious cause of their king and country that they suffered. But not to treat with levity a subject so very serious, let us take another example; the poor soldier, who at the conclusion of a long war, reduced by famine, sickness, and fatigue, and disabled by cruel wounds, is finally compelled to drag on a miserable existence in an hospital, or a work-house; or is returned upon the wide world, without hope, and void of expectation, a burden to himself, and useless to all around him. It would be pale and sickly consolation to his drooping spirits, to be informed that his were wounds and sufferings worthy of a soldier and a man, because they were acquired in his country's cause. Humanity must weep over victory when purchased upon such terms, and tremble for the fatal effects of desolating war, whereby immediate misery is occasioned to thousands, and eventual sorrow inflicted upon millions.

> What hope for man! o'erwhelming war,
>   Uncommon furies in his train,
> O'er heaps of carnage rolls his car,
>   And Europe mourns her thousands slain:
> What hope! amidst disastrous days
>   *When freedom's temple totters to its base,
> And with earth's vilest brood dishonoured science
>   strays†.

The author, in his beautiful ode, has finely introduced this apostrophe, to the unfortunate situation of his country, involved in a calamitous and destructive war abroad; and its happiness and tranquillity subverted and destroyed at home by the real or pretended existence of plots and conspiracies, it matters not which, for they are equally to be lamented; because they have, in either case, been the cause of suspending the great bulwark of English liberty, the Habeas Corpus Act; and of giving rise to many arbitrary measures, which nothing but the most absolute necessity could justify. He has also expressed his indignation at that severity of punishment, almost unequalled in history, which was inflicted upon two men, whose real intentions *deserved applause* instead of disgrace.††

* Alluding to the suspension of the Habeas Corpus Act, and to the fate of Muir and Palmer.

† Ode on a distant prospect of Cambridge.

†† The author of these letters does not mean to throw out any reflection upon the criminal laws of England. It is well known that the law which banished Muir and Palmer for fourteen years, composed part of the Scotch jurisprudence. The author is convinced that the *common law* of this land is its greatest glory, that it is a sword to the guilty, and a shield to the oppressed; and that as long as the *Habeas Corpus* Act remains unviolated, and the *trial by jury* pure and independant, no time or tyranny can ever efface the liberties of his country.

27

The well of the virgin St. Winifred is well known for its singular virtue of curing the blind, the lame, and the palsied. Innumerable are the trophies of old crutches, wheel-barrows, spades, &c. that decorate this venerable building; the grateful testimonies of those various cures which its miraculous waters have performed. The story is as follows:

'St. Winifred, a beautiful and devout virgin, having fled from a young man called Cradock, the son of a king named Alane, who would have dishonoured her, he pursued and overtook her near the church, where, on her refusal to yield to his desires, he with his sword cut off her head. On the spot where it fell, there suddenly sprang up a fair well, yielding a vast quantity of exceeding clear water, yet famous for its wondrous virtues in healing diverse diseases; at the bottom of the well are to be seen stones spotted with blood, which stains, cannot be effaced, and round its sides grows moss of a marvellous sweet odour.

'St. Bueno, a holy man, coming from the church to the spot where the body lay, and finding the murtherer, who had not power to move from thence, he first replaced the head, and then by his prayers raised Winifred to life, and struck Cradock suddenly dead, whose body turning black, was instantly conveyed away by fiends; soon after St. Bueno going to Ireland, ordered St. Winifred to send him an annual token, which was to be put on the stream of the well, from whence it would be carried to his place of residence, fifty miles beyond the sea.'

Rudland is remarkable for its castle. The founder, as well as the precise time in which it was founded, is quite uncertain. It is situated upon the banks of the Clwyd.

Abergeley is a small watering place, about half a mile from the sea.—They have a strange custom there, that has an air of great indelicacy to a stranger; which is, that the inferior orders of people commonly bathe, without the usual precautions of machines or dresses; nor is it singular to see ten or a dozen of both sexes promiscuously enjoying themselves in the lucid element, regardless, or rather unconscious, of any indecency. Not being myself accustomed to this mode, I chose to retire farther up; but it is very unpleasant bathing, being a flat level beach, and necessary to wade a quarter of a mile into the sea before one can arrive at any comfortable depth.

The approach to Conway, from the opposite side of the water, is extremely grand. The castle (built by Edward the First, A.D. 1284) stands upon a rock, the foot of which is washed by 'Conway's foaming flood.' I there paid a visit to the tombs of my ancestors, some of whom lie buried in the church belonging to the town. Observe that this visit must not be attributed to superstition, or ought of peculiar veneration for their memory, but the effect of mere curiosity; for there is a singular monument of one of them, who was the father of forty-one children, by two wives. I took down the inscription with a pencil, and then left my prolific ancestor to his uninterrupted repose.

We strengthened our party at Conway by the addition of two of our particular acquaintance, whose plan being similar to our own, we united our interests, and set out from Conway, each provided with a stick, knapsack, and trowsers. We certainly presented to the astonished Cambrians a very formidable appearance; sometimes exciting their risible muscles, and sometimes being the occasion of much alarm, particularly amongst the children, who always took us for Frenchmen; but the country

29

people, in general, looked upon us as recruits. Our walk to Abber was singularly beautiful; this road was formerly almost impassable, but with incredible labour and expence, it has of late years been rendered more commodious. The deep and gloomy passes between the stupendous mountains, that seemed ready to close over our heads, had an appearance truly terrible and grand; and almost induced me to give credit to what Cambden has asserted,—that two shepherds might converse together upon opposite mountains, and be a day before they could meet. The pass of Paenman Mawr, that was once attended with so much danger to the wary traveller, is now perfectly safe. We arrived late in the evening at Abber, which consists but of three or four houses; the inn is very commodious, but, at the same time, the accommodations are rather extravagantly purchased. We rose early the following morning for the purpose of ascending to the top of Paenman Mawr, and ordered dinner to be ready for us at two o'clock, expecting to have returned by that hour; but we reckoned without our host, for the expedition took up nearly the whole of the day, and we thought ourselves happy to return when we did.—We rashly took the resolution to venture up this stupendous mountain without a guide, and therefore unknowingly fixed upon the most difficult part to ascend, and consequently were continually impeded by a vast number of unexpected obstructions. At length we surmounted every danger and difficulty, and safely arrived at the top; but the fatigue we had undergone, and the excessive heat of the day, deprived us, in a great degree, of that pleasure we should otherwise have received from the prospect, and occasioned a tormenting thirst that we were not able to gratify; for water was an article which we searched for in vain. Preparing, in the utmost despondency, to descend, we accidentally turned over a large flat stone that concealed a little spring, which, thus obstructed, became absorbed under the surface of the earth. The parched-up soldier of Alexander's army could not have felt greater joy in the discovery of his little treasure, than we did of ours. In the course of our descent we incautiously separated; and as it was dusk, I began to be under some apprehension that we might lose ourselves in the intricacies of the mountain; in order to discover their direction, or distance from me, I frequently repeated their names, and was much entertained with a beautiful echo, which returned the sound of my voice in three different directions; had I been inclined to superstition, many circumstances would have contributed to raise its full effect upon my mind, which as it was, busily employed itself in creating images of fear. An awful silence succeeded the last vibrations of the echo, which was only interrupted by the distant barking of the watch dog, that proceeded from the lonely hut of the shepherd; or the shrill shrieks and hootings of the owl and rock eagle.—In the midst of my melancholy cogitations, I fully expected that the genius of the mountain would have appeared to me in some formidable shape, and have reproached me with rashly presuming to disturb the sacred silence of his solitary reign; or at least that some banditti, more terrible in aspect than ever Salvator Rosa could have painted, or even imagined, would have rushed upon me from behind a rock, and made me pay, perhaps with life, for my unintentional temerity. We had the good fortune, however, to arrive at the inn together, nearly at the same time, that is to say about nine o'clock. You may easily imagine that the difficulties we had previously encountered, heightened the enjoyments of our present situation, and we passed a very pleasant evening in discoursing upon the adventures of the day. There is a cataract about a mile from Abber, worth seeing, on account of its precipitous fall; but it is totally destitute of wood or scenery. This evening we meant to cross the ferry

into the Isle of Anglesea, but I will reserve the account of this part of our journey until another opportunity, or till the experience of new adventures may render a repetition acceptable.—In the mean time believe me, my dear friend, under every circumstance of time or place, I shall still continue my best wishes for your happinesss, and remain
Your's sincerely, &c.

I.H.

LETTER IV.

CAERNARVON, July 19, 1794.

SINCE my last, my dear friend, I have encountered some difficulties both by land and water, and am, in consequence, come to a final determination in my own mind, that terra firma is infinitely preferable to that changeable element where Neptune holds his powerful sway. I must acknowledge the dangers of the latter are not by any means so agreeable, nor can I view them with that tranquillity which, upon most occasions, I have treated the former; not indeed that I am blessed with any great share of philosophy, although I am always toiling to acquire a little of that necessary ingredient to human happiness; but alas! the irritation which such exercise has upon my nerves, is so hostile to the object in view, that it drives philosophy to a very respectful distance. In the uncertain voyage of life, some sail upon troubled, others on smooth and gentle waters, and some again on stagnant; and it is our duty to expect to encounter all sorts of weather: man is at the best but a weak being, like a reed to be shaken by every wind, and buffeted about by every storm; some are better sailors than others, and look upon the angry tempest with different degrees of fortitude; for my part I must honestly confess that I am at the best but a bad navigator, and am often run ashore with only a cap full of wind.

32

The following anecdote which I have accidentally met with, is so singular, that I cannot refrain from sending it to you:

A merchant who lived in the golden days of Queen Elizabeth, had seven or eight sons arrived at the age of manhood, and being himself upon his death bed, addressed them as follows: 'Sons,' said he (after some previous discourse), 'your voyage through life may be compared to an outward bound fleet in time of war, that has a safe convoy to a certain latitude, where they usually separate, and take different courses; some navigate one sea, some another, and naturally meeting with various fortunes, one encounters storms and tempests; another runs upon shoals and quicksands; and a third, even in sight of port, strikes upon a rock, and is lost; whilst few, very few, smoothly sailing upon the tranquil tide, gain their destined haven in peace. So, my sons, I, your convoy, have conducted you even thus far with honor and safety to yourselves: I must now leave you for ever, in all probability to be scattered wide by many fates; let each, whatever course he may steer, have virtue for his pilot, and I trust that his faithless fortunes—;' but here the story breaks off, and so must I, in order to make an apology, which, according to the polite rules of writing should now follow, for this unnecessary digression.—And methinks I hear you say, I am travelling 'tis true; but it is into the regions of fancy, beyond the reach of common apprehensions; I allow the justice of the charge, and stand self convicted; but I find it a very hard task to keep within due bounds: for, to pursue the allegory—in the course of a voyage, if the master of the vessel happens to discover a beautiful island, abounding with all sorts of fruit, is he a criminal, or even an injudicious pilot, if he is tempted to deviate from his direct track, in order to gather some? Or if he hears a Syren's voice, is he to blame in listening to it? when

33

to resist, the expedient of Ulysses would be insufficient—he must also shut out the imagination.

The village of Abber Conway, usually called Abber, from whence I dated my last letter, is situated upon the straits of the Menai, that at high tide is there about four miles across; but when the water is out, it appears perfectly dry; for the sea retires so far back, that it only leaves a channel of a quarter of a mile, or thereabouts, in breadth: all the rest is a complete flat, and consequently the tide overflows it very rapidly. There are stated times to pass this ferry, which one should be very exact in observing, for ten minutes may be of the utmost consequence. The clergyman of the place accompanied us to the boundaries of this wilderness of sand; he gave us the necessary directions for our passage, which were only to keep a white house in view that belonged to the ferryman on the Anglesea shore, and to make what haste we could, since there was no time to lose, for we had four miles to walk over this frightful desart without shoes or stockings, having been advised to pull them off; for being regularly overflowed every twelve hours, great part of the road is necessarily wet and dirty. We had scarcely got half way, before it began to grow thick and foggy. The little village of Abber, which we had just quitted, was no longer perceptible; and nothing behind us was to be seen, but the steep and shaggy mountains of Paenman Mawr, and those known by the general name of Snowdonia, with the dark vapours floating upon their sides; and very soon even these became no longer distinguishable, but as one huge mass of clouds. Myself, and another of the party, had considerably outwalked the other two, who had lost sight of their landmark, and were steering their course much too far to the right; when we discovered their mistake they were not so visible to us, that we could tell what they were; all that we could discern, was something very dark, moving in a different direction to us; consequently we haled them, and waited till they came up to us, and we agreed to part company no more.—Darkness had now overtaken us in good earnest, and we could see nothing, nor hear any thing, except the noise which the sea made in its approach, that alarmed us not a little; at length, to our infinite satisfaction, we distinguished the voices of the ferrymen, who were luckily waiting on this side of the passage. When they heard us, they were extremely impatient for our arrival, and continually called to us to make haste, which we wanted no monitor to urge us to do; we therefore made towards the spot from whence the sounds came, which we conjectured to be about the distance of two hundred yards from us, but were unluckily intercepted by a small channel, already filling very fast with the sea. We did not hesitate long, for in fact we had no alternative, and therefore boldly ventured through; it was fortunately only about two feet deep, and rather more than ten yards broad. We congratulated each other upon finding ourselves safe in the boat, though dripping wet, and shivering with cold. Like the Israelites, we had passed through the sea on dry land; but we had run a great risk of experiencing a similar treatment with Pharaoh and his host, from that unmannerly element. When we arrived at the inn at Beaumaris, we made a fire that would have roasted an ox, and ordered a supper sufficient for ten aldermen. Upon opening the window on the following morning, I observed the sea had covered all those immense flats we had so lately, I will not say with dry feet, walked over.

The first Edward, ambitious of emulating the actions of Alexander the Great, entertained the daring project of building a bridge across these straits, and thus unite Anglesea with Wales. That proud monarch, like the insolent Xerxes, vainly conceived he could control the raging elements; and the trouble, expence, and impracticability of completing so vast a work, was clearly, but in vain, represented to him: chance, however, effected what reason had been unable to do; for at the very time that he was giving orders for the undertaking, some fresh disturbances broke out elsewhere, and diverted his attention from so wild and visionary a scheme.

Beaumaris is a dirty sea-faring town; here is another of king Edward's castles built, A.D. 1295; it is in tolerable preservation, but the eye is disgusted with new repairs; a fine old tower is frequently patched with modern masonry, in which the workman has barbarously shown his art, in the nice disposition of yellow bricks and mortar: add to this, the inhabitants have made a bowling-green within its walls.—The guardian genii of venerable ruins, must surely have been asleep when these impieties were committed.

From Beaumaris we crossed the island, with which I felt myself greatly disappointed; I looked around me in vain for those awe inspiring shades and venerable temples where the Druids used to perform their mysterious rites, that filled the wondering multitude with fear, and infused, even into their enemies, a degree of respect and veneration.

The account given by Tacitus of the expedition of Suetonius, against this island, is the most striking picture of the character of the Druids, and probably more to be relied upon than any other; for veracity constituted no small part of the merit of that excellent historian.

*'Igitur monam insulam incolis validam, et receptaculum perfugarum aggredi parat. . . . Stabat pro litore diversa acies, densa armis virisque, intercursantibus feminis: in modum furiarum, veste ferali, crinibus disjectis, faces praeferebant.

* Tacit Annal Lib. 14.

Druidœque circum, preces diras sublatis ad coelum manibus fundentes, novitate aspectus perculere milites, ut quasi haerentibus membris, immobile corpus vulneribus praeberent. Dein cohortationibus ducis, et se ipsi stimulantes, ne muliebre et fanaticum agmen pavescerent, inferunt signa, sternuntque obvios, et igni suo involvunt.'

'He thereupon prepares to attack Mona, an island powerful on account of its numerous inhabitants, and affording a place of refuge to those who fled from the enemy. . . . a motley army stood opposed to him upon the shore, thronged with warriors and prepared with warlike instruments, the women running up and down, and bearing torches before them, after the manner of the furies, in the dress worn at their funeral solemnities, and with dishevelled hair; the Druids every where pouring forth the most dreadful imprecations, with hands uplifted to heaven, terrified the soldiers with the novelty of such a spectacle, who, as if fixed to the spot where they stood, yielded their bodies immoveable to the wounds of their enemy. At length, at the exhortations of the general, and also encouraging each other, that they should not be intimidated at that female and frantic multitude, they advance their standards, overthrow all who oppose them, and plunge the Britons into their own fires.'

By the bye this last was an act of the most unjust and unnecessary cruelty in the Romans, who seem only to have been instigated to it by the demons of revenge; for when we consider that the deluded multitude who opposed their invasion, were in reality fighting in defence of every thing that was valuable in their domestic, and of every thing that was dear and venerable in their public life; that they beheld the temples of their gods impiously polluted, and their sacred groves violated and profaned; can we feel surprised, or rather was it not natural that

37

they should resist the fury of an enemy, preparing to trample upon their rights, their liberties, and their religion? And if in general, we regard the conduct of the Romans with respect to the conquered nations, we shall find that the most cruel and rapacious spirit characterised all their military transactions. They led the unhappy victims of their persecution in barbarous triumph to the capital, and felt a more than brutal pleasure in listening to the groans of the untaught and defenceless children of nature, the naked inhabitants of the wilds and forests of the most uncivilized and unpromising regions. Their inhumanity and cruelty is only to be equalled, in more modern times, by the conquest of Peru and Mexico, and the taking of the island of St. Domingo by the Spaniards, which has fixed an indelible blot of infamy upon that nation; and by that disgraceful and abominable traffic that subsists to this day in the West, of bartering our fellow creatures at a public auction, and subjecting them to the disgraceful dominion of the most unfeeling of tyrants.

Very few traces of the temples and habitations of the Druids are now to be found; some old stones, shapeless and without order, here and there, indicate that there might have stood on these spots the rude and simple piles, where the primaeval inhabitants of this island solemnised their religious ceremonies; and this is all that now remains of that once celebrated order of priesthood, which overspread the northern regions of Europe. Strange fatality! that a system of religion so founded on prejudice, and rivetted in superstition and ignorance, and so intimately blended with the political governments of those times, that it appeared capable of triumphing over that invisible mutation to which all human establishments are liable, and of opposing Christianity itself, should now be so lost, so forgotten, that little more than a few shapeless stones, and the uncertain testimony of oral tradition, remain to satisfy us of the influence that extraordinary religion once possessed over the human mind:

'Illi rebus divinis intersunt, sacrificia publica ac privata procurant, religiones interpretantur . . . fere de omnibus controversiis publicis privatisque constituunt, si quod est admissum facinus, si caedes facta, si de hereditate, si de finibus controversia est iidem decernunt, praemia paenasque constituunt.'*

'They preside over all sacred ceremonies; they administer both public and private sacrifices; they are the interpreters of all religious affairs. . . . They for the most part decide in all public and domestic controversies; if any crimes are committed, if any slaughter is made, whether they are disputes concerning hereditary right, or the boundaries of their possessions, the Druids always decide upon them; they also determine rewards and punishments.'

This is a general account given by Julius Caesar of the Druids of Gaul. He slightly mentions those of Britain; only taking occasion to observe, that the manners and ceremonies of these people are almost every where the same. Their powers of divination were also in great reputation, but the mode of making their observations was truly horrid and barbarous. Their ceremonies, according to Tacitus, were performed 'in groves, sacred to the most cruel superstitions; for they offered up their sacrifices upon altars stained with the blood of their captives; and it was usual for them to augur according as the blood of the human victim followed the sacred knife that had inflicted the wound.'

Anglesea (though it is called the granary of Wales) appeared to us as one continued picture of desolation; and for twenty miles of our road through it, we could not discover more than five or

* Caesar in Gall, Lib. 6.

six corn fields, and the grass land so miserably poor, that it starved rather than fed its hungry inhabitants. We undoubtedly did not see the country to the best advantage, because the excessive heat of the summer had parched up the ground, and occasioned a general appearance of dearth.

Amlwch is a small sea port, from whence the copper (that is found in the Paris and Mona mines, which are not more than a mile from the town), is shipped to London, Liverpool, &c. The Mona mine produces the finest ore; they also make quantities of copper from old iron (for a particular account of the whole process, see the Scotch Encyclopedia, Pennant's History of Wales, &c.)

These mines have an appearance uncommonly grand and striking—a vast yawning chasm, displaying full to the view of the astonished stranger its sulphurous contents; hundreds of workmen employed in a variety of different occupations; some boring shafts, others selecting the ore, which is slung up to the top, or, if I may use such an expression, ushered into the world in little baskets. In some places the chisel and the pick-axe find room for employment; in others the men are sedulously engaged in blowing up large pieces of the rock by means of gunpowder, the report of which reverberating from side to side, in this immense cavity, occasions such a tremendous explosion, that all nature seems to tremble to its center.—Upon the whole these mines bear an apt resemblance to the infernal regions, and, like the pestilence from the pit of Acheron, the sulphur which issues from them, spreads desolation around, so that not the slightest vestiges of verdure are to be traced in the neighbouring fields.

We dined yesterday at Gwyndn, on the great road to Holyhead, which is called by the natives Caer

40

Guby, on account of St. Kybi, a holy man, who lived there A.D. 308; but none of us expressing any inclination to see that place, we left it on the right, and steered our course nearly South, through the center of the island. Gwyndn signifies, from its name, a place of hospitality at the expence of the lord; and, in truth, it answers, in some respects, to its title even now; nor must I forget to pay my tribute of thanks to the hostess, a fine old lady, who payed us the utmost attention, and appeared particularly solicitous about us; she gave us her blessing at our departure, with a thousand admonitions not to lose ourselves. We left this hospitable inn with regret, and arrived 'post multa pericula,' at Hoel Don Ferry, a single house, where we were obliged to sleep, or, speaking more accurately, to lie down, for to sleep was totally impossible. It was a miserable hut; but we contrived to procure two beds, though the good woman was for putting us all into one. We crossed the ferry yesterday morning, after a sleepless night, happy to quit this inauspicious island, where fortune had not been over prodigal to us of her favours. The road from this ferry to Caernarvon, winds along the shores of the Menai, and the scenery would have amply repayed me for the fatigue and mortification I had undergone, had I then been in a humour to have enjoyed it; but true it is, that when we cannot enjoy ourselves, we are not much disposed to be satisfied with any thing around us; the finest objects lose their beauty; and what at other times would have afforded the highest gratification, are in those hours deprived of their relish. We reached Caernarvon, or Caer-ar-fon (signifying a walled town), to breakfast; and it was not until I had eaten, or rather devoured, a certain quantity of toast and butter, that I began to recover the accustomed tone of my spirits. I intended to have closed this letter with an account of our transactions as far as the time of our departure from this place; but must defer the remainder till my next, for some

41

particular business has fallen upon my hands, which obliges me for the present to subscribe myself,

Your's, &c.

I.H.

LETTER V.

Tan y Bwlch, July 24, 1794.

Of all the ruins which Wales has yet presented to me, the castle of Caernarvon is the most noble and magnificent. 'Vast as the pride of its founder,' it evinces the warlike and invincible genius of the first Edward, of whose military prowess this country, as well as Scotland, furnish such numerous and melancholy proofs. Thank heaven, these fabricks of despotism are at length either levelled with the ground, or present a memorable lesson to mankind of the futility of human ambition.

This castle was erected in order to secure the passage into the Isle of Anglesea, and to curb the people of the mountains, where the brave and hardy Britons had taken refuge from their insulting conquerors, resolved to prefer freedom and independance to ease and servitude. The eldest son of Edward was born here, and he was presented to the Welsh as their future prince. Such enormous buildings, abstractedly considered, excite only my abhorrence; because they have occasioned the exercise of a great deal of tyranny, and useless expence, and have been of no possible advantage to any nation; but have, on the contrary, afforded so many asylums wherein the sword of tyranny might take shelter; and were chiefly calculated to keep the surrounding districts in awe and subjection. Every castle that now remains is a monument of shame to our ancestors, and of the ignoble bondage under which they bent: and hence in part arises that satisfaction, which the mind is conscious of feeling, in contemplating their ruins; for an association naturally takes place; and the recollection of the feudal vassalage and slavery of former days, is accompanied by the pleasing circumstances of the relative prosperity and freedom which we now enjoy. From this place we made a party of three, and crossed once more into Anglesea, where my ill stars seemed to have pre-ordained that I should meet with nothing but misfortunes. One of my companions was a very skilful botanist, and his botanical furor induced him at all times to despise danger and difficulty, when in pursuit of a favourite plant, and this was the object of our present enterprize; but we had scarcely set foot on that inhospitable shore, before it began to rain with great violence, and very soon growing dark, we were obliged to make the best of our way back again. This ferry is two miles across, and the water was much agitated, so that without the addition of the rain, which came down in torrents, the spray of the sea would have completely made us wet through; but, in the midst of our distress, we were agreeably interested by a sight as beautiful to us as it was novel; the surface of the water suddenly assumed a luminous appearance, now and then relapsing into an impenetrable gloom, and then again re-lumined, it conveyed to the mind some idea of what the poets describe of Phlegethon in the shades below. By the time we had reached our inn I had lost my voice, and gained a sore-throat; the following morning it was no better; but under some hope that exercise would cure the complaint, was induced to continue our tour to Bethkelert, which we reached that afternoon; the whole walk being more singularly romantick than any I had yet seen, and compelled us to make many a pause, in order to enjoy and contemplate its beauties. About half way, we passed over Llyngwennyn bridge, and immediately found ourselves in a fertile valley, terminated by a wild and irregular cascade, one branch of which contributed to turn a mill that was almost concealed within the wood, which formed a kind of amphitheatre to this picturesque and interesting scene; a little further on a fine lake opened full upon the view; and not far from this another smaller one. The road winds along the banks of both. Bethkelert is a small village, or rather hamlet, situated at the foot of some prodigious high mountains, which seem to encircle it on all sides, whilst the stream or torrent, that had accompanied us all the way from the first lake, here begins to be of more consequence, and forcing its way between these stupendous hills, with a continued and considerable descent, empties itself into an arm of the sea, called Traweth Mawr. As this is the usual place from which travellers make the ascent of Snowdon, we determined to do the same, and in pursuance of this resolution set off at eleven in the evening, though it was quite dark, and a very rainy and stormy night; however, there was a probability that it would be fine in the morning; and that hope was sufficient to make us undergo a few inconveniences; but in attempting to find the guide's house, which was five miles from our inn, and situated quite out of the road, at the foot of the mountain, we became completely bewildered: in this perplexity we were directed by the glimmering of a light to an habitation, which, with extreme difficulty and danger, we contrived to reach. It was a small hut, and its inhabitants, if we might judge from the impenetrable silence that reigned within it, were all asleep. It was some time before we could prevail upon them to open the door, and answer to our entreaties for a proper direction; at length an elderly man appeared, to whom we endeavoured to make known our grievances; but alas! he only spoke his native language, and did not understand a word that we said: However, by frequently repeating the guide's name, 'Ellis Griffith,' and pointing to Snowdon, at the same time giving him a glimpse of a shilling, we

44

with much difficulty made him comprehend us; and putting himself at our head, he became our conductor. In about half an hour we found ourselves at the door of another small cottage: our guide vociferated Welsh for some minutes, till we were admitted by a good-looking lad about 17 years of age, who was the person we had been searching for: he remonstrated against our ascending that night, with many weighty reasons, to which we easily assented; but to think of returning to our inn would be madness: we therefore called a council of war, and it was agreed, that we should at all events stay where we were, until morning; when, if it should be tolerably fair, we would ascend. Thus determined, we disposed of ourselves in the following manner; I barricadoed myself in a chair, so that I could not fall out; two more reposed themselves on the benches on each side of the fire, and the fourth took up his "lodgings on the cold ground," with an earthen platter turned up-side down for his pillow. As for my part I was not disposed to sleep, but took up the rush-light, which had been placed for security on the ground; and to pass away the leaden hours of time, pored over an old Welsh dictionary (which was the only thing like a book that I could find), till I was scarcely able to see. I could not help contemplating our singular situation and appearance in this strange place: on one side, around the dying embers of a peat fire, my good friends were enjoying as comfortable a repose as they had ever experienced in the most costly bed: at the other extremity of the room, separated only by a rug, the venerable owners of this humble cottage lay locked in each others embraces: whilst I, like Brutus in his tent at Philippi, sat reading by the mid-night lamp, till the light danced before my eyes, and the pale spectre of the night appeared to my imagination. Without doors nought but the 'pelting of the pityless storm' was heard, and the loud roar of the mountain torrents: I recollected some lines of a favorite

45

author, which I thought applicable to my present situation:

> 'And when rude blust'ring winds and driving rain,
> Prevent my willing feat;
> Be mine the hut that from the mountains side
> Views wild and swelling floods.'
>
> COLLINS.

Yet while I was contemplating the scene, under such peculiar circumstances, with a mixture of awe and surprise, these simple cottagers lay perfectly indifferent, and unconscious of any novelty in their situation. The noise of the cataract was by them scarcely ever remarked, or served to strengthen their repose; mountain floods, abrupt and broken precipices, were alike viewed by them with the utmost indifference; so soon does the human mind become familiar, and accommodate itself to any circumstances. Habit and custom are even so powerful as to change the very complexion of things, and render that finally pleasing, which at first could not be viewed without fear or dislike. The Savoyard will climb from rock to rock, and fearless walk upon the brink of tremendous precipices, which we, unaccustomed to such scenes, cannot contemplate, even at a distance, without emotion; but, in a little time, we become familiar to them, and ridicule those fears we had formerly entertained, for what we can now view with so much unconcern.

At four in the morning I thought it prudent to awaken the whole party, which I effected with some difficulty; we then sallied from our habitation, and made our observations upon the weather, which gave us no encouragement to proceed; however, they determined to venture upon their aërial excursion, more from the hope of finding the plants, for which this mountain is remarkable, than of seeing any thing when at the top: at their persuasions, added to my own inclination, I declined the enterprise, as my cold had considerably increased during the night, and went back again to the inn, where I impatiently expected their return, which did not happen till four in the afternoon. It turned out, as might have been foreseen, a fruitless and fatiguing expedition; for when arrived at the top, they could see nothing but the impenetrable clouds, that almost constantly envelope these huge mountains.

We quitted Bethkelart the following morning, and pursued the course of the same stream I have above spoken of; that for nearly two miles rolls with great rapidity at the foot of prodigious high mountains, which rise on each side of it, almost perpendicular from its banks, leaving but barely room for a narrow road, which must have been cut at a vast expence. The gentle and murmuring sounds of the water, occasioned by its declivity, and the obstructions it has to overcome, form a rude but grateful harmony. Pont Aber Glaslyn terminates this sublime scene. The bridge, and surrounding objects, are here highly deserving of attention. From hence we steered our course to the left, and traversed the wildest and most desolate country that North Wales can boast of; for the most part consisting of vast hills, rising one above another, covered with shaggy rocks, without the slightest vestiges of verdure. We reached this place yesterday evening: I am delighted with the situation, which is the most retired and pleasing I have ever seen; it stands upon the borders of a valley sufficiently high to command a view of its whole extent; the Druryd, a small, but interesting stream, winding its solitary course, undisturbed, through the midst of it; and, at the lower extremity, a simple, but elegant bridge, terminates the view. The woods are very picturesque, and cover the opposite hills to a great extent; gratifying the eye with a constant variety. Why, my dear friend, has nature placed her most alluring haunts, her most delightful scenes, so far from the reach of man?

47

Why has she prodigally squandered away upon so many distant and uncivilized regions, and upon this favoured country in particular, all her majesty and simplicity? Why has she given to a people, who behold, without enjoyment, scenes of beauty, where, for my part, I could be almost content to pass through this strange scene called life, in peace and solitude? I know you will blame me for thus giving way to visions, which ought not to be realized, and your answer I already anticipate (viz.) that man was not made for solitude, or selfish enjoyments. That our brother travellers, through this tedious journey, call for our assistance, and have a claim upon our exertions; and that nature would no longer please, no longer afford delight and gratification in her works, if they were every where equally beautiful; or, in other words, were there not barren mountains, smoky cities, ungenial soils, and unwholesome climates; then would lakes, woods, rivers, fertile valleys, cultivated plains, villages, and hamlets, be no longer objects of curiosity or admiration.

The inn at Tan y Bwlch is remarkably neat and commodious; we yesterday made an excursion from hence, to view the fall of the Cynfael, one of the most celebrated cataracts in Wales. With much difficulty and danger I climbed up to its tremendous and almost unattainable summit; from whence the water, collected into a body, falls tumbling from rock to rock, and steep to steep, till it reaches a vast pool, or bason, frightfully deep, and so remarkably clear, that the pebbles at the bottom of it may be distinctly perceived, though I could form no judgment of its depth. The scenery at the foot of the cataract, was beyond imagination beautiful; but I will not attempt to give you a particular description of it, because I have neither time nor power to do it justice. We leave this place to-morrow morning, and you may conclude, after what I have said, it will be with sorrow and regret. I shall now close this long, and I fear, tedious letter, and be assured, I feel myself as much as ever,

Your sincere Friend,

I.H.

LETTER VI.

ABERISTWITH, July 29, 1794.

THIS is the last letter, my dear friend, that I shall have the pleasure of writing to you whilst I am in Wales; an unexpected event obliges me to be at Bath in a few days, so that I am under a necessity of leaving this country sooner than I had intended; but I will take care and write to you as soon as I arrive, with the remainder of my tour, together with a few observations upon the character of the people.

It was with much difficulty we found our way to Harlech. We made some enquiries at a small village, but in vain; for though we addressed ourselves to many, we could by no means make them understand us; all we received in return was a stare, immediately followed by a grin, and concluded with a 'tin sarcenick,' which signifies 'no Saxon.' We were obliged therefore to rely upon chance for our guide, which did not however upon this occasion befriend us; for, instead of keeping to the right upon the hills, we pursued the left path, that brought us into an extensive vale, or marsh, where, at the distance of about five miles, we first perceived the objects we were in pursuit of (viz.) the town and castle of Harlech. After some considerable exertions, we were obliged to abandon this valley, because it was so swampy, and so much intersected by ditches and drains, that it would have been, if not impracticable, at least extremely uncomfortable and difficult to proceed. With great fatigue and perseverance, we climbed up the almost perpendicular, and craggy sides of the mountain, which

49

bounded that part of the vale, where we were reduced to the above perplexity, and at length reached Harlech; for the first time heartily fatigued.

The country people have no idea that a stranger can be ignorant of their roads; we have not unfrequently asked the way, and received for answer, 'that it was as straight as we could go;' when, in a very few paces, we have been perplexed by two roads, one declining to the right, and the other to the left.—Nor have they much idea of distance; each measuring it by the rule of his own judgment and opinion. It is no unusual thing to be told, that the distance to such a place, may be about five miles, 'and a pretty good step;' which pretty good step, generally proves to be about five miles more.

Harlech castle is nobly situated, and, like Denbigh, stands upon a lofty promontary, terminating a chain of hills, and commanding on one side 'a view of the sea, and on the other, a very extensive vale and prospect. From its singular situation, it must have been formerly esteemed almost impregnable; and yet we read in our history, that it was besieged, and taken, in the time of Edward the Fourth, by the Earl of Pembroke, without the assistance of gunpowder. We also here achieved an exploit, which, beyond all doubt, gives us some title to military prowess; for as there did not happen to be any body in the way, who might open the gates of the castle, and our time not permitting us to wait for the ordinary forms of capitulation, we boldly marched up to the assault, and scaling the walls at four different places, took possession of the garrison, as it were by a coup-de-main. But for this daring outrage, we had well nigh got into an aukward scrape; some of the inhabitants observing our operations, and probably taking us for free-booters, gave the alarm; and mustering a formidable body of forces, marched in military array, to dispossess us of our strong hold. But we soon pacified our opponents, and having convinced them that our intentions were neither predatory nor hostile, they retired to an ale-house to banish sorrow, and indulge themselves, at our expence, in copious libations of ale.

There is nothing interesting in the road to Barmouth, nor has that place itself any striking peculiarities, except that the houses are so whimsically built, upon the side of a steep hill, that the inhabitants may have the advantage, if they choose, of looking down their neighbour's chimneys. The town stands upon the sea shore, and in the season is full of company, who resort thither for the purpose of bathing.

From Barmouth to Dolegelly we were highly gratified; the road wound along a ridge of rocks, that hang over the Avonvawr, an arm of the sea; which, at full tide, has the appearance of a large lake, surrounded with beautiful woods: The mountains on both sides, but particularly on the opposite shore, were strikingly grand; and above all, Cader Idris reared its head into the clouds, which, together with the sombre aspect of the evening, and the hollow murmurings of the sea gave an awful sublimity to the scene that cannot be described.

Dolegelly is a large and dirty town: we took up our quarters at the Golden Lion, a good hospitable inn; and next morning, after breakfast, procured a guide to conduct us to the top of Cader Idris. We armed him with stores, and warlike preparations of all kinds (to wit): ham, fowl, bread, and cheese, and brandy, and began the ascent at nine in the morning, and continued to toil for three hours and a half before we reached the top. But, alas! expectation had again flattered us; for, though it was a most lovely day in the valleys, yet here we could not see

51

fifty yards before us; the summit of the mountain is not of greater extent than the base of a common sized room; and, on one side, falls almost perpendicularly many hundred yards in depth. When I stood upon the edge of this precipice, and looked into the frightful abyss of clouds, it put me in mind of the chaos, or void space of darkness, so finely described in Milton, when the fallen archangel stood at the gates of hell, pondering the scene before him, and viewing, with horror, the profound expanse of silence and eternal night:

> . . . a dark
> Illimitable ocean, without bound,
> Without dimension, where length, breadth, and
>   heighth,
> And time, and place are lost.

The height of this mountain is little inferior to that of Snowden.—The view from it, on a clear day, is grand and magnificent. Ireland, the Isle of Man, North, and South Wales, lie extended before the eye like a level map. The whole mountain is apparently composed of a huge mass of stones, thrown together as a heap of rubbish without order or design; for, wherever you turn up the sod or turf, which is not in general more than two inches thick, you come to these stones, and they are nearly about the same dimensions, and have the appearance of being broken with a hammer. Near the summit of the mountain there is no turf, and what is remarkable, these stones are smaller there than in any other place. Had there been any larger massy rocks at the top, it would have afforded a probable conjecture, that shivered in the course of time, by lightenings and tempests, they might have fallen by piece-meal upon the lower sides of the mountain. But, as I have already stated, there is no appearance of that kind at the summit, and such a supposition must therefore be excluded. Nor could an earthquake have caused the phenomenon, because we have no testimony whatever, either ancient or modern, of any part of Great Britain, having been subject to such extraordinary convulsions of nature; and the idea of the flood being the cause, is futile and ridiculous to the last degree; for the vast body of water, which, we are informed, was collected upon the surface of the earth would, instead of scooping out valleys, and heaping up mountains, have been more likely to have levelled mountains, and filled up valleys. Besides it is not quite clear, that the whole surface of the globe was affected by that sweeping deluge; and therefore Great Britain, from its remote situation, might, as well as any other country, have been exempted from a share of its favours. But it is not my intention to throw down the gauntlet of controversy, with respect to this, or any other subject of scripture history so extremely remote; it is happy perhaps for the authenticity of many parts of that history, that it is beyond the reach of human testimony now to disprove it.

It is well for me, my dear friend, that I do not live under the paternal government of the inquisition, either in Venice, or Spain, or Italy, or Portugal, or any other place, where the parental and tender affection of the holy fathers, might solely for the preservation of my soul, mercifully condemn my body to the purification of fire. But to return to the mountain, or rather to take leave of it, for I have already kept you too long upon so ungenial a soil, I will conclude this digression, with the idea of a celebrated philosopher, who conceived it probable, that, when God had compleated his great work, this beautiful world, out of so many rough materials, not knowing what to do with the rubbish that remained, he threw it together in various heaps of different magnitudes, just as it happened, and thus formed what we call mountains.

We arrived at the inn, at Towen Merionith, late

53

in the evening; where we had the pleasure of being spectators of a Welsh assembly; they invited us to join them, but our fatigue was too great to permit us; added to which our dress was not altogether suitable to the occasion; though, from what I could observe of these honest Cambrians, we should not have been very outre in our appearance, if we had ventured amongst them, habited as we were. I cannot help relating a remarkable instance of simplicity, that happened to me here the same evening. As soon as I had got into bed, I found the sheets were extremely damp, and having suffered so much lately in catching cold, I thought it a necessary precaution, and indeed but common prudence, to throw them aside. When the maid came to take away the candle, she would not be convinced that the sheets were damp: 'Lard sir (said she), it be impossible, for they have been a slept in four or five times within this last week.' We left Towen (which is about a mile from the sea), yesterday morning, for there is nothing particularly attracting in that place, or captivating to the eye of a stranger. It was our intention to have reached Aberistwith last evening, but were obliged to take shelter from the fury of a storm, in a solitary house, not far from the ferry at Aberdovy, where we were detained much against our inclinations the whole night; but we have happily arrived here this morning without any further obstacles. Aberistwith is a very respectable bathing place. There are some fine remains of a castle, that formerly commanded the approach from the sea on one side; and that to the town, from the land on the other.

The trade of Aberistwith is not by any means contemptible; great quantities of coal, and lead, are found in the neighbourhood, and shipped from this port to different parts of England.

Adieu, my dear sir, and believe me, I feel the

greatest pleasure in subscribing myself,

Your sincere friend, &c.

I.H.

LETTER VII.

THE OLD PASSAGE, August 2, 1794.

IN my last, my dear friend, I said that you would not hear from me until I reached Bath; but I find I shall be detained here till the morning, the weather proving too rough for the passage boat, to venture with their cargo of live and dead stock, and therefore I cannot better fill up the intervening time than by writing to you.

I did not part from my old companions until we reached Llanindovrey, so that we had the pleasure of seeing Pont-ar-finach together, otherwise called the Devil's bridge. It is the largest cataract in Wales, and well worth the traveller's attention. About one hundred yards from the bridge, there is a house of accommodation for company, though I cannot say much in favour of it; however, it is pleasantly situated, and overlooks the deep and woody glen, into which, from a prodigious height, the waters of the cataract fall, with a deafening noise. With infinite labour and fatigue, I got down to the bottom of this glen, or chasm. I did not undertake the perilous expedition alone; but neither my companion or myself were gratified or recompensed for our trouble, because the cataract is so obscured by bushes and underwood, that, at the foot of it, it is not all discernible.

Tregarron is a miserable hole, in the which however we were constrained to sleep, and to break the windows in our bed rooms to let in the fresh air. We took a guide from thence to Llanindovrey, over the lonely and trackless mountains of Cardiganshire; it rained hard the whole way, and we had not even the gloomy consolation of seeing a partner of our misfortunes: for, to speak within compass, we neither beheld a single habitation, nor even a human creature, for more than twenty miles. From Llanindovrey I journeyed on alone, for the rest of the party not being pressed for time, could make their observations at pleasure, having no necessity for hurrying over the country as I was obliged to do.

Brecknock is situated on a small rising, above the river Usk. I cannot do justice to the beauty of the country, the whole way from Brecknock, to Crickhowel and Abergavenny: it is one continued landscape, abounding with every rich variety of scenery, and beautifully interspersed with hamlets and villas. At Crickhowel there are some remains of a castle, but at Abergavenny (commonly pronounced Aberganey), scarcely any: it derives its name from the river Gavenni which there meets the Usk. To me, who had but just quitted the uncultivated and tremendous scenery of North Wales, its rocks, its mountains, and its cataracts; the fertile hills and cultivated vales of Brecknockshire were doubly striking; and the rich features of the latter, heightened beyond the reality from so lively a contrast.

Ragland castle is a very fine ruin, belonging to the duke of Beaufort; the road from thence to Tintern, would gratify the most romantic imagination; the last three miles, or more, being a continual descent through a deep and gloomy wood, till the astonished traveller bursts from the surrounding scenery full upon the Wye, that rolls its muddy waves in rich meanderings through this solitary glen. The lively picture that immediately offers itself to the view, of boats in full sail, of others landing their cargo, with the busy and cheerful cries of the sailors and workmen, was like the effect of enchantment, and almost created in me an imagination, that I had arrived in another world, and had discovered a new order of beings. At some distance stands the abbey, whose holy isles, and melancholy shades, were once devoted to religious fervour and monastic discipline: it was founded A.D. 1131. The monks were of the rigid order of Cistertians.* We owe to Henry VIII the suppression and overthrow of these seminaries of bigotry and superstition: as long as they existed, the exertions of genius were fettered and confined; and Europe was overspread with one general gloom of religious fanaticism and intolerance. About the twelfth and thirteenth centuries, some enlightened minds awoke from the general slumber; but it was a feeble effort, and the darkness returned more thick and heavy than before. Monkish pride and cloistered pedantry every where usurped dominion over man.—Learning and science were finally depressed, and ignorance became the best shield of protection; but truth at length unfolded the deep veil of hypocrisy and priestcraft—reason resumed her empire—the whole

* At what time christianity was introduced into Britain, it is not correctly known; but it is certain that it was in some degree established here, though continually persecuted by the Saxon Pagans, long before the arrival of Augustin the Monk, who was sent upon a holy mission into this island, A.D. 596. However, the abuses of christianity were coeval with its introduction; and this holy father himself set his heart not only on spiritual but temporal things; for he was created the first archbishop of Canterbury: he is also accused of having excited the Saxons to fall upon the Britons, and to massacre twelve hundred monks of Bangor. Monachism is supposed to have been introduced into Britain by Pelagius, at the beginning of the fifth century.

The contracted limits of a note are insufficient to enumerate the infinite variety of monkish fraternities, and the crimes they were guilty of: but according to Gregory, their enormities are scarcely credible. In consequence of the suppression of these monasteries in the time of Henry the Eighth, ten thousand religious were turned into the wide world; and Henry became possessed of all monastic revenues whatsoever; these on the whole amounted to six hundred and forty five monasteries, ninety colleges, and two thousand three hundred and twenty four chantries and free chapels.

fabric of papal despotism fell at once to the earth; and lust, cruelty, and revenge, that had so long been concealed within its walls, fled at the first glimmerings of light; whilst the pure and genuine principles of Christianity rose as a pillar of glory upon the ruins, and pointed to universal happiness and peace.

The elegance and lightness of the structure exceeds any thing of the gothic architecture I ever saw. It occasioned in me much regret that I was compelled to pass over, and to visit, in so cursory a manner, a scene, which, for beauty and singularity, might challenge nature throughout. I wished to have examined more minutely the venerable remains of this once celebrated abbey; but the very fabric which I was so much admiring, indicated too forcibly that I had to deal with that inexorable and insatiable foe, called 'Time.' I felt the conviction, and with reluctant steps hastened to Persfield, celebrated for those extensive and magnificent gardens, which have cost so much labour and expence heretofore, though now suffered to run into decay.

Chepstow is a very neat and well situated town; it has a castle that might once have been formidable, but is now a complete ruin. Having thus brought my tour to a conclusion, I have the satisfaction to add, that the event has not disappointed, or fallen short of expectation; and what few difficulties we encountered greatly contributed to heighten our other enjoyments. 'Tis true we have sometimes been obliged to cook our own victuals, sometimes to be content with very scanty fare, and sometimes with none at all; nor were we ever indulged with down beds, chince curtains, or Turkey carpets; but good health and wholesome fatigue rendered such articles of luxury totally useless and unnecessary. To sum up the advantages and disadvantages; I do not hesitate a moment to say, that were I to make the same tour again, or one through a similar country, I should certainly perform it on foot, both from motives of convenience and independency.

Upon the whole I have been as much charmed with the manners of the people, as with the country which they inhabit; there is a boldness and original- ity in all their actions, which marked the conduct, and characterised the features of their ancestors. A love of liberty and independence is implanted by nature in their breasts, and is cherished into matur- ity upon their mountains and sea coasts by a hardy and desultory manner of life. With respect to hospitality, they still preserve their original charac- ter; the manner of it is undoubtedly much altered, it is less magnificent but more pleasing; the stranger is not conducted into a noble hall, and placed at the right hand of the chief; no bards attend with the songs of times that are past; the walls are no longer hung with the massy spears of departed heroes, or decorated with the spoils of a vanquished enemy; the conch does not sound to war, nor is the bossy shield struck as the signal to meet the threatening foe. Strange ferocious manners were blended with the hospitality of those days; but, happily for mankind, such barbarous features of uncivilized ages are at length every where humanized into more refined and social enjoyments. Whether society has not arrived at an excess of refinement; whether a great degree of refinement is not the parent of vice and corruption; and if so, whether an age of barbar- ity with honesty and virtue, or an age of refinement, with effeminacy, vice, and corruption, is most desirable, or most calculated to produce the immediate and eternal happiness of mankind? I leave to be determined by those who have leisure and inclination, to consider with attention so abs- tracted a subject.

The occupation of war, and the amusements of

the chase, have given way to the more domestic employments of pasturage, agriculture, and fishing.—Of the produce of their daily labour, the stranger is generally welcome, and though their poverty is obvious, they refuse every recompence but thanks and civility; I speak chiefly of the lower orders of the people; of the higher, or more opulent, the manners are almost every where the same.

I cannot do better than quote, upon this occasion, a couple of stanzas from Churchyard, who has been a constant companion in my walks, and has better expressed in poetry the character of the people in this particular, than I could have done, had I attempted it, in prose:

> Like brethren now doe Welshmen still agree,
> In as much love as any men alive;
> The friendship there and concord that I see,
> I do compare to bees in honey hive;
> Which keep in swarme and hold together still,
> Yet gladly showe to straunger great good will;
> A corteous kynd of love in every place,
> A man may find in simple peoples face.
>
> Passe where you please on plaine or mountain
>   wilde,
> And bear yourselfe in sweete and civil sort,
> And you shall sure be haulst with man or childe,
> Who will salute with gentle comely port
> The passers by: on braves they stand not so,
> Without good speech to let a trav'ler go:
> They think it dett and duetie franke and free,
> In towne or fielde to yeeld you cap and knee.

In Wales, pride and poverty go hand in hand, and the disposition of the people is strongly blended with superstition. When we were at the top of Cader Idris (the etimology of which signifies the chair of the giant Idris), the guide shewed us the giant's bed, at which we could not help laughing; the honest fellow, however, rebuked us for such levity, and expressed his belief as to the identity and existence of the giant, at the same time justifying himself from the authority of a clergyman, who had lately made a pilgrimage to the same spot; and, immediately falling down on his knees, began to say his prayers in a devout manner, and an audible voice; without doubt to appease the manes of this tremendous giant, and breathe out a pious requiem to his soul.

The general character of the people is certainly amiable—their attachments are strong and sincere; their passions and resentments violent, but transitory, which is always the characteristic of an unpolished people. The ingenuousness of nature is shewn in its real colours, and displayed in all their actions. They do not trouble themselves with the politics of the times, or addict themselves to the habits of thinking, and the cares of the world they have little concern with; for they are free from those occupations, those tremulous solicitudes, which engross the attention of a commercial people. With respect to their language, I am not sufficiently acquainted to give any opinion; to my ear, I must confess, it is not very harmonious; but resembles rather the ravishing sounds of a cat-call, or the musical clack of a flock of geese when highly irritated. The dialects are extremely various, and the difference is often observable, even between adjacent counties; but in North and South Wales, there is so great a variation that they may almost be said to be different languages. Yet, notwithstanding, I feel much pleasure whenever I hear it spoken, being the old Celtic dialect, which, together with the simplicity of the country people, brings back to my mind the memory of former times; but my ideas of them are so imperfect, and our knowledge in general, of the relative virtue and happiness of our Celtic ancestors, so confused, that I scarcely know whether to rejoice that those times are past, or wish that they may again return; with respect to them, and the Welsh, as they are at this day, there appears to me to be this material distinction: the former knew not what wealth (in the modern acceptation of the word) was; and consequently were strangers to many vices attendant upon it. The latter, from their intercourse with the rich and mercantile parts of Great Britain, have unfortunately acquired a relish for riches without the means of procuring them: hence arises that pride which prompts them to conceal their poverty, and the jealousy of their national character and situation, which breaks out almost upon every occasion. The children are remarkably beautiful, and usually well made, but this only continues during their infancy; for, from the age of ten and upwards they begin to bear the marks of hard labour, and still more precarious subsistence.—A haggard countenance, a reduced appearance, and, in short, all the traces of a premature old age:* sad proofs these of poverty and

* Poverty, though it does not prevent the generation, is extremely unfavourable to the rearing of children; the tender plant is produced, but in so cold a soil, and so severe a climate, soon withers and dies. It is not uncommon in the Highlands of Scotland, for a mother who has borne twenty children not to have two alive. Very few of them arrive at the age of thirteen or fourteen; in some places one half of the children born, die before they are four years of age; in many places before they are seven; and almost every where before they are nine or ten. This great mortality, however, will be found chiefly amongst the children of the common people, who cannot afford to tend them with the same care as those of better station.

Adam Smith's Wealth of Nations.

This excellent writer, whose calculations are in general so accurate and exact, has here stated facts the most melancholy, truths altogether disgraceful to society; hard lot of poverty indeed! and blasted is the soil, if its influence extends to the untimely and unmerited destruction of the human race. The stale and hacknied argument, that these things are permitted by Providence for some wise purposes unknown to man, must in this instance be rejected, because it is apparently a levity of cruelty, to give a numerous offspring to the parent, only to mock and insult her with a prospect of happiness, and then leave her to anguish and despair.

Great Britain is enabled to provide for more than its present population, even without the assistance of any external commerce. And Europe, it is well known, might maintain one hundred millions of souls wretchedness; and but too true indications of misery and want, and of an inferiority of condition, justifiable upon no grounds whatever, either of revealed religion or natural equity. The population of North Wales, compared with its extent, is very trifling, and unequal. This may be accounted for from a long chain of causes, but chiefly from the continual state of discord and warfare, in which the chiefs and princes were always involved, until the final subjugation of Wales by Edward the First, and even then, the inhabitants were treated merely as a conquered people, and admitted to few privileges of the conquerors; for it was not till the time of Henry the Eighth, that they were suffered to have the same advantages with English subjects. Secondly, from the situation of the country, which is too remote for the English land trader, and opposed to a very dangerous sea; added to which its ports are by no means so commodious and safe as those of England. Thirdly, and principally, the barrenness of the soil, together with the mountainous nature of the country, and consequently the great difficulty of land carriage, which is the chief obstacle to its internal trade. These are certainly serious impediments to the flourishing state and prosperity of the people; but they are not beyond a remedy, and it ought to become the duty of the legislature to provide every possible means of improvement, and to endeavour, by wisdom and attention, to remove or diminish those local inconveniences which are a bar to the happiness of the society of any particular district or tract of land over which that legislature has dominion; establish manufactures, hold out rewards for agriculture; in short, increase the population of the country by the most approved methods; wealth will

more than she at present does. Government then is the only remaining cause of all these evils: government, which ought to remove every obstacle to population, endeavours to depress and retard it; nor is there any hope of amendment, while amongst numerous other causes, the abuse of estates, the rapacity of finance, and the immense establishment of standing armies continue to exist.

follow of course, commerce will be extended, and the now desolated mountains of North Wales may, at least, repay the labour of cultivation, though they can never be so productive and flourishing as those of their southern neighbours. We know that Attica was little better than a desart of sand; yet, encouraged by wise laws, the inhabitants overcame the obstructions of nature, and it quickly flourished as the garden of Greece. We know the almost insurmountable obstacles that the great Czar Peter had to encounter; yet, in spite of these, affluence smiled upon the industrious exertions of his subjects, directed by his wisdom to useful employments: the arts found an asylum in the frozen regions of Russia, and, from a land of poverty and desolation, it became a great and flourishing empire; but the sole end of governments seems to be forgotten, and, instead of having for their great and ultimate object, the happiness and advantage of that society by whom they were instituted; they now seem calculated only for the advantage of a few; and the legislators of nations are become the individual brokers of public property; which, with the lives of mankind, are squandered away, as ambition or caprice may rule the hour, and dictate to their councils.

You will perceive, my dear friend, that I have not entered into minute and particular descriptions—I have neither given you a detail of sieges, nor presented you with a genealogy half a mile long—I have not described a feast, nor filled up my pages with inscriptions from old tomb stones; but if you wish to derive information on these heads, I refer you to the pompous descriptions of Young, and to the diffuse and voluminous work of Pennant. The world is doubtless indebted to the latter for his excellent history of Wales, but it is still a history, and has too much of the detail in it to afford me any gratification in the perusal.

I have studiously avoided dwelling upon any thing which bore an analogy, or resemblance to works of art, or unproductive ambition. To search out nature in all her various forms, has constituted my chief delight; and to find her in her wildest attitudes, has proved to me the highest source of gratification and enjoyment.

I hope, and fully expect to see you very soon at Cambridge. My best wishes attend you, and believe me to be, with the utmost sincerity,

Your affectionate Friend,

I.H.

Appendix

IT may not be unacceptable to some of my readers, to lay before them a few general observations with respect to this country.

NORTH WALES

IS DIVIDED INTO SIX COUNTIES.

	Contents in square miles.	Towns.	Parishes.
Caernarvonshire	430	5	68
Denbighshire	670	4	57
Flintshire	250	2	28
Merionethshire	790	4	37
Montgomeryshire	860	6	47
Anglesea	180	2	74
	3180	23	311

The market towns in Caernarvonshire, are Carnarvon, Aberconway, Krekith, Pulhely, and Nevin. It has besides one city, Bangor.

In Denbighshire, are Denbigh, Ruthin, Wrexham, and Llanrost.

In Flintshire, Holywell, and Caerwis, with one city, St. Asaph. Flint has no market, but sends one member to Parliament.

In Merionethshire, are Harleigh, Dolgelle, Dinasmouthy, and Bala.

Montgomeryshire contains Montgomery, Llanvilling, Welshpool, Newtown, Machynleth, and Llanydlos.

66

Angelesea has Beaumaris, and Newburgh.

No. of square miles in Wales	7011
Ditto in North Wales	3180
Ditto in South Wales	3831

The population of North and South Wales, are together estimated at about three hundred thousand souls, so that it will appear there are not upon the average, quite forty-three inhabitants to each square mile. I regret much that I have not been able to learn the exact proportion of population between North and South Wales; there is, however, no doubt that the latter has by much the largest share. The Isle of Anglesea contains fifteen thousand inhabitants, and has rather better than eighty three to each square mile; but it is the most populous part of the north division of our principality. The total amount of the waste lands in Wales, is computed to be about 1,629,307 acres, and great part of this is stated to be incurable; but I am inclined to believe that if two or three regiments of soldiers (instead of spending in barracks a life totally unproductive to themselves, and useless to society in every instance, except for the heroic and benevolent purposes of murder, rapine, and oppression), were set to work upon them at a shilling each per diem, exclusive of their pay, the country would, in a short time, assume a very different aspect. The price of labour is greater in South, than it is in North Wales, and yet in Caermarthenshire, which is a southern county, labourers are only paid ten pence a day in summer, and find their own diet, and eight pence in the winter months. The land tax a few years ago produced 43,752 l.

There are numerous mines of coal, slate, copper, &c. that are a great source of employment to the poor.—What trade they have, is, for the most part, inland, and consists chiefly in horned cattle, lead, copper, and coal. Great part of the land, and particularly in Cardiganshire, is wild pasture, and, in its present state, only fit to feed that hardy kind of cattle so peculiar to the country itself; consequently sheep, cows, &c. are very cheap, and will continue so until agriculture flourishes more than it does at present; or, in other words, until it becomes more profitable to extend tillage, and sow seed for the food of man, than dedicate the rude and natural produce of the earth to the nourishment of cattle; for, in proportion to the extension of agriculture, the price of cattle will be advanced, because the number is thereby diminished, and the demand for them greater. The Welsh are probably descended from the Belgic Galls, and hence called Galles, or Walles, *i.e.* Strangers. The country was also formerly inhabited by three tribes of Britons, the Silures, Dimteæ, and Ordovices. It preserved its independency until the thirteenth century.

There are two circuits, viz.

| North East | } containing { | Flint, Denbigh, Montgomery, |
| North West | | Anglesea & Caernarvon. |

Wales sends twenty-four representatives to parliament, twelve for the counties, and the same number for the boroughs.

If the traveller wishes to see Bangor, he must cross the Menai from Anglesea at the Bangor ferry; but we had been informed that there was scarcely any thing worthy of particular notice at that place, which account has been since confirmed to me, by a gentleman with whom I am well acquainted, and who, in company with some others, made a similar excursion to our's, and in a similar manner. It is from his notes that I am enabled to give some account of Llanberis. The road from Bangor to Llanberis is over some stupendous mountains, commanding, as one might have expected, a very extensive, and not an uninteresting prospect. The vale of Llanberis may contend the point of superiority, with respect to beauty, perhaps with any in Wales; the mountains on one side being entirely without verdure, and rising almost perpendicular from the vale, whilst those on the other side appear to be highly cultivated; the vale itself consisting mostly of fine pasture ground, some small lakes at one extremity, and a few rustic cots at the other; here is also a copper mine in the hands of the Macclesfield company. From Llanberis to Caernarvon, which is about ten miles, the road lies at first over high and unpleasant mountains, and is afterwards succeeded by a low flat, equally dull and disagreeable.

Eight miles from Dolegelley are the falls of the Caen and Morthway. The highest part of Snowdon is called the Wyddfa, from whence, according to Pennant, its most credible altitude above the level of the sea, is one thousand one hundred and eighty nine yards. The height of the Cader above the green at Dolegelley is about nine hundred and fifty yards. The road to Machynleth, by the pool of Three Grains, is for the most part picturesque and beautiful. The town, for a Welsh one, is rather neat; from hence to Aberistwith, is a pleasing and rich country, through which flows the river Dovey.

There is a remarkable custom which the Welsh still continue, that I cannot forbear mentioning: When a marriage is about to take place amongst the middling and lower orders of people, it is usual to invite all their friends and relations of every description, who, when they take leave, present the bridegroom with some small present, of one or two shillings, which, however, they have a right to demand again after a certain space of time; the intent of it being probably to enable the new married couple to buy stock, or engage in some business that may allow them soon to repay the small donations of their friends. It is called 'a bidding,' and is drawn up in the following form.

'My only son John has lately entered the sacred state of union, and a bidding is fixed on the occasion, on Tuesday the 7th day of October next, in the village of Conwyl, when and where your good company and benevolence are highly solicited, which will be cheerfully acknowledged on a similar occasion, and esteemed a peculiar favor conferred on,

Your most devoted

humble Servants,

John Jones, Senior.
John Jones, Junior.

Conwyl,
Sept. 13, 1794.

P.S. Mr. and Mrs. Lewis, of Pantyrhaidd, Mr. Jones, of Clynadda, Mr. Evan Harries, of Nant-yr-olchfa, and his brother, David Harries, of Llandre, unite us in complimenting all with their sincerest gratulation.—The young man's parents request that all their donations of the above nature may be retaliated then.'

In the course of our tour I had often occasion to regret that I knew nothing of drawing; the pencil may find room for continual employment in the romantic views of North Wales; but without professing myself either a poet, a painter, or a botanist, I felt highly gratified at the magnificent scenery which that country every where displays. Equally delighted with the elegant simplicity of nature, but not so familiar with its productions as another, I cannot find the same sources of intellectual acquisitions. Undoubtedly the antiquarian and the botanist

70

have a wider field of investigation, and a more enlarged page of science is constantly displayed to their view. The poet and the philosopher are more abstracted in their observations, find other principles for the materials of thought, and apply the rude unconnected objects of their contemplation, as so many foundations, upon which to build the light fabric of fancy, either in the regions of moral, political, or metaphysical speculation; but where these are united, nature must amply repay her observer, and be at once an inexhaustible mine of information and amusement.

A
LIST
OF
TOWNS, &c.
WITH
THEIR DISTANCES FROM EACH OTHER.

CAMBRIDGE	0
Oxford, three weeks	90
Glocester*	47
Ross*	16
Hereford	12
Leominster*	16
Bishop's Castle*	25
Montgomery	7
Welsh Pool	9
Llanvilling*	12
Llangunnog	8
Bala*	12
The Druid House*	8
Corwen	$2\frac{1}{2}$
Llangollin	$9\frac{1}{2}$
Ruabon	7
Wrexham**	5
Ruthin	16
Denbigh*	8
St. Asaph	6
Holywell*	11
Rudland	11
Abergeley*	5
Conway*	11
Llanaber, or Abber**	9
Over the Ferry to Beaumaris	5
Amlwch*	18

72

THE END.

Notes on the Text

p. 1 Epigraph adapted from lines 50–54 of Book I of *The Minstrel or The Progress of Genius* by James Beattie (1735–1803), Book I being published in 1771, Book II in 1774. The original reads:

> Liberal, not lavish, is kind Nature's hand;
> Nor was perfection made for man below.
> Yet all her schemes with nicest art are plann'd;
> Good counteracting ill, and gladness woe.
> With gold and gems if Chilian mountains glow;
> If bleak and barren Scotia's hills arise;
> There plague and poison, lust and rapine grow;
> Here peaceful are the vales, and pure the skies,
> And freedom fires the soul, and sparkles in the eyes.
>
> (lines 46–54)

Beattie, a Scot, was Professor of Moral Philosophy at Aberdeen University: *The Minstrel* enjoyed widespread popularity and was for a time a highly influential work. The Revd. Richard Warner in *A Walk Through Wales in August 1797* (1798) quotes from it several times.

p. 2 *some fresh calamity*: Britain's military fortunes were at a low ebb during 1794–5. The autumn of 1794 saw her forces falling back behind the Meuse, leaving the French in possession of southern Holland; in December Frederick Duke of York was relieved of his command, and the British retreated in disarray into Germany, to be evacuated home in 1795. During the course of the year Tuscany, Prussia, and Spain, partners with Britain and Austria in the First Coalition against France, made peace; at home there were bad harvests which resulted in food riots throughout the country.

p. 3 *tautology and egotism*: cf. Coleridge's Preface to *Poems on Various Subjects*, 1796: 'Compositions resembling those of the present volume are not infrequently condemned for their querulous egotism. But egotism is to be condemned then only when it offends against time and place, as in an History or an Epic Poem. To censure it in a Monody or Sonnet is almost as absurd as to dislike a circle for being round . . .'

p. 4 *'Travels' History'*: *Othello* I. 3. 139.
'most disastrous chances' etc.: *ibid.*, I. 3. 134–5.

p. 5 *we have not fatigued ourselves with very long marches*: the present-day reader may have decidedly different views on the subject; by his own reckoning Hucks covered 629 miles on the tour, excluding the journey from Bristol home to Exeter, in a space of some fifty days, not all of which were 'walking days'. (See the *Itinerary*, p.113 below.)

<table>
<tr><td>pp. 6–7</td><td>*'O how can'st thou renounce'* etc.: see note on title-page above. Hucks is quoting from Book I of *The Minstrel*, lines 73–81.</td></tr>
</table>

p. 10   *a few poor sheep*: Norman Freeman, *Coleridge, the Damaged Archangel* (London, 1972), p. 299, compares with this passage lines 29–32 of Coleridge's *Reflections on Having Left a Place of Retirement*, first published in October 1796, line 30 of which reads 'The bare bleak mountain speckled thin with sheep', but the resemblance is not close enough to prove that Coleridge borrowed the image from Hucks.

the *'Man of Ross'*: John Kyrle (1637–1724) who devoted his adult life and modest fortune to improving the amenities of Ross-on-Wye, and performed numerous acts of philanthropy and benefaction still remembered in his native town, where his house, once The King's Arms, stands in the market-place. His generosity was celebrated by Alexander Pope in *Moral Essays III: Epistle to Bathurst* (1733), lines 249–290.

'Richer than misers' etc.: Coleridge's poem was first transcribed in his letter to Southey from Wrexham, 13th July 1794 (see Appendix I below), and was published with slight variants in the *Cambridge Intelligencer*, 27th September 1794. It appears in *The Complete Poetical Works of Samuel Taylor Coleridge*, ed. E. H. Coleridge, 2 vols, Oxford 1912, (hereafter referred to as *Poetical Works*), I. 57.

p. 11   *Powis castle*: now thought to have been built c. 1250 by Owain ap Gruffydd, Powis Castle was much restored in the 16th and 17th centuries.

Cadogan ap Bledhyn . . . his nephew Madoc: Cadwgan (d.1111, prince of Powys) was the second son of Bleddyn ap Cynfyn; after a turbulent career he was treacherously slain at Welshpool by his nephew Madog ap Rhiryd, who had killed Cadwgan's brother Iorwerth the previous year.

p. 12   *Verniew*: now Vyrnwy.

ycleped: the use of archaism here reminds one that Hucks in his *Ode to Pity* (*Poems*, pp. 59–67) expresses admiration for the work of Chatterton:

> The youth forlorn, who struck the lyre
> To dauntless Ella's sprite of fire,
> And lov'd, with rapturous hand to spread
> The wild weeds round stern freedom's head. (lines 29–32).

(cf. Coleridge's *Monody on the Death of Chatterton*, first published in 1794.) Chatterton committed suicide at the age of seventeen in 1770.

p. 14

'*to mix their heads with dropping clouds*': we have been unable to trace the source of this quotation.

We were yesterday much diverted etc.: Coleridge's letter to Southey of 13 July and that to Martin of 22 July present a different picture from that outlined by Hucks, in which the toast of 'General Washington' was pronounced by one of the 'Welch Democrats' and not Coleridge (see *Introduction*, p.lxi). Hucks also omits the reconciliation which appears to have taken place between the travellers and three of the four village worthies. (See Appendix I.) (See also Fruman, *op. cit.*, pp. 18, 445 note.)

p. 15

the two Arrans: Aran Mawddwy (2970') and Aran Berllyn (2901').

p. 17

castle Dinas Bran: literally 'the fort of the crow', an eighth-century fortification situated on a conical hill above Langollen, to the north.

p. 18

Cramer . . . Clementi: Johann Baptist Cramer (1771–1858) was a celebrated pianist of the day, the son of Wilhelm Cramer (1743–1799), London violinist and conductor; he studied under Clementi from 1782–4, thereafter winning international celebrity. Muzio Clementi (1752–1832) was an Italian-born pianist and composer, who settled in England in 1782, and was a fashionable teacher and performer in London for the next twelve years.

risum teneatis amici: forbear to laugh, friends.

p. 19

the dark figures of the miners: coal mining is still an important industry in East Clwyd, formerly Denbighshire; it has been carried on in the Ruabon district for over 500 years, but only developed significantly from the mid-eighteenth century onwards.

Chirk castle: built by Roger Mortimer in 1310 and occupied continuously since that date, the castle has been the home of the Myddleton family since 1595. One of its features is a pair of magnificent wrought-iron gates, completed by the brothers Davies in 1733.

Winstay: Wynstay, near Ruabon, the seat of the Wynn family.

Mr. Middleton: in 1794 Chirk Castle was the seat of Richard Myddleton, who died in the following year; he was Lord Lieutenant of Denbighshire and M.P. for Denbigh. His son, also Richard, died unmarried in 1796.

Sir Watkin William Wynne: Sir Watkin Williams Wynn III (1772–1840) who succeeded his father Sir Watkin Williams Wynn II (1749–89), and whose brother Charles (1775–1850) was a lifelong friend of Robert Southey.

a bridge where the two roads meet: Pont-y-Cysyllte.

p. 20

some remains of a castle: Ruthin Castle was built in 1281 and

demolished by order of Parliament in 1646; the modern castle
was constructed in 1826–52. When Hucks and Coleridge visited
it, the castle had been neglected for some 130 years.
'*This delightful vale* etc.': quoted from pp. 171–2 of *A Gentleman's Tour Through Monmouthshire and Wales* (1775) written by
Henry Penruddock Wyndham after his tour in June and July
1774. Wyndham traversed Wales in the reverse direction to
Hucks and Coleridge, and made a more sustained exploration of
the country, much of it undertaken on horseback.

p. 21   *the castle*: Denbigh Castle was built between 1282 and 1322 by
Henry de Lacy, Earl of Lincoln, and his successors. In the Civil
War it withstood a six month siege when held for the king, until
it was surrendered in October 1646, when it became a prison.
Churchyard: the poet Thomas Churchyard (c. 1520–1604) was a
contributor to *A Mirror for Magistrates*, being responsible for the
accounts of Cardinal Wolsey and Shore's Wife. In 1587 he
published *The Worthiness of Wales*, an account of the history and
topography of the principality; Hucks probably carried a copy of
Thomas Evans's reprint of 1776 with him on the tour (see p.xlii
above, and note to page 87 below).

p. 23   '*sounds of heavenly harmony*': possibly a reminiscence of Dry-
den's *Song for St. Cecilia's Day*, 1687, lines 1, 11.
Corporal Casey: Coleridge in his letter to Southey of 13 July
refers to the tune of *Mrs. Casey*, and in his letter to Martin
quotes two lines of the words:

> The British Lion is my Sign—
> A Roaring Trade I drive on &c.—

(see Appendix I).

lines upon Denbigh castle: Hucks's poem was printed in his
Poems, pp.101–104. That version, which departs from the text
originally published, runs as follows:

> *On the Ruins of Denbigh Castle, in North Wales*
> Now sad and slow, borne far on dusky wing,
> Sails the still Eve—Night from her ebon throne
> Slow rising, scatters wide her mystic spells
> O'er the tir'd world; and from yon murky cloud
> Gleams the pale moon, diffusing holy light
> Thro' many a midnight Isle and silent scene.
>
> Much musing on this mimic round of life,
> And all it's strange vicissitudes, I view
> Proud Pile! thy tempest-beaten towers, that rear
> Their heads sublime, and to the angry storm
> Bid bold defiance, tho' their aged brows
> Bear visible the marks of stern decay;
> While superstition, with a phrenzied eye,
> And wildering fear, that thro' the shadowed gloom

Kens many a horrid form and spectre pale,
Affright the lonely wanderer from thy walls.
Proud Pile! engraven on thine aged front,
In deep but time-worn characters, I trace
The stern feudality of antient years:
Ambition reared thee in an evil hour,
To cover it's dark doings—many a tear
Thy walls have witness'd!—many a tortured groan
Appall'd the silence of thy midnight gloom!
Is there a heart that sorrows at thy fall?

Ye patriot few; who arm'd with fortitude,
E'er while have fought for freedom! whom the force
Of England's proud usurpers, nor their threats
Could even bend from virtue's stern resolve!
For what ye have done, ev'n with tears of joy
Now do I thank ye; 'tis the only need,
I have to offer, humble, but sincere.
I thank ye for that lesson, which your deeds,
Bright as the richest gem in virtue's crown,
Have taught me—deep engraven on my heart
In life's ingenuous spring, 'twill never die.

Far hence thou busy world! nor here intrude
Thy sounds of uproar, arguing much of care,
Of impotent alarms and deep dismay
Of hateful contests, hopes, and sickly fears.
Stop traveller! and with mournful eye behold
Which time and desolation have assail'd
With wildest havock—O'er the solemn scene
In silence pause—It is the pictur'd tale
Of man's brief hour; ev'n as this mouldering pile,
That yet lifts high its forehead to the storm,
Till the wild winds shall tear it from it's base;
So flies the date of poor mortality;
For while man journeys, heedless, thro' the vale
Of many-colour'd life; with silent tread
Time, yet unknown to pity or to spare,
Steals on his path, and sweeps him from the earth.

p. 25   *'reckless that age and sorrow'* etc: Mr. Anthony W. Shipps has
kindly traced Hucks's source to William Lisle Bowles's
'Monody, Written in Matlock' (1791), lines 151–2 of which run:

> Reck not how age, even thus, with icy hand,
> Hangs o'er us . . .

p. 27   *What hope for man!* etc.: Hucks quotes from his friend William
Heald's poem *Ode on a Distant Prospect of Cambridge*, 1794 (See
p.xxv above). Poems by Heald were published in Hucks's *Poems*
of 1798, pages 171–89.
suspending the great bulwark of English liberty: the Habeas Corpus

Act was first suspended 'in the national interest' in 1794, and thereafter annually until 1801. Thomas Muir and Thomas Fyshe Palmer were sentenced to transportation for fourteen and seven years respectively after grossly unfair trials in 1793 during the 'Dundas despotism' in Scotland, when political reformers were regarded as seditious and ruthlessly supressed.

p. 28

The well of the virgin St. Winifred: St. Winefrid (variously Winefride, Wenefrida, Gwenfrewi, Guinevra), an actual historical figure, died c. 650 A.D., and is said to have been the niece of St. Beuno. Tradition has it that she was murdered by Caradog of Hawarden after refusing his advances, but another version of the legend suggests that St. Beuno restored her to life and she became abbess of Gwytherin, Clwyd.

The story is as follows: we have been unable to trace the source of Hucks's account.

Rudland is remarkable for its castle: Rhuddlan Castle on the east bank of the river Clwyd was begun by Edward I in 1277 to command the estuary and its important anchorage, as well as the main coastal road into North Wales. It was by the Statute of Rhuddlan in 1283 that Edward granted Wales its judicial rights.

p. 29

They have a strange custom: cf. Coleridge's letter to Martin (Appendix I). Sea-bathing does not appear to have come into vogue until after the middle of the eighteenth century, and although both sexes bathed naked for some time after this, it was the practice at fashionable resorts to separate them, and for the bathers to have recourse to machines.

The castle . . .: Conwy Castle, a magnificent example of mediaeval architecture, was built by Edward I between 1283 and 1289 to command the mouth of the river. In the Civil War it was surrendered to Parliament in 1646, and subsequently fell into disrepair, being substantially restored in the nineteenth and twentieth centuries.

'Conway's foaming flood': see Thomas Gray's *The Bard*, line 16. Richard Warner, *op. cit.*, pp.155–6, remarks 'On considering the character of this stream, which has nothing 'foaming' in it, we were immediately struck with the impropriety of Mr. Gray's epithet for it . . . had he written from actual observation, he would have known its features are of the opposite kind, and that it meanders in peace and silence through the vale'. But had Richard Warner explored the *upper* reaches of the Conwy, he would doubtless have accepted Gray's epithet as accurate, even though the poet (who never visited North Wales) was not working from first-hand knowledge of the river.

the tombs of my ancestors: See *Introduction*, p.ix above.

two of our particular acquaintance: from Coleridge's letters (see Appendix I) we learn that the two Cambridge students who joined Hucks and Coleridge in Conwy were Brooke and Berdmore, both, like Coleridge, of Jesus College. John Brooke, born on 28 January 1773, was educated at schools in Bury and Norwich, and entered the college as a sizar in October 1790. In the following year he was made Scholar of Jesus College, and graduated B.A. in 1795, proceeding M.A. in 1798. From that date until 1811, he was a Fellow and Tutor of the college. Ordained Deacon in 1795 and Priest in 1800, he served as Vicar of Whittlesford, Cambs., from 1807–21, and Vicar of Elmstead, Essex from 1810–21, dying on 23 November 1821. Thomas Berdmore was the son of Dr. Samuel Berdmore, Master of the Charterhouse from 1769–91, at which school he was educated. He was admitted to Jesus College as a pensioner on 24 June 1791 but elected a Scholar in the same year, graduating B.A. in 1795, becoming a student of Lincoln's Inn on 15 April 1795. (Information from Venn, *Alumni Cantabrigiensis*, Pt. II, Vol. I)

trowsers: trousers were only gradually coming into ordinary use by the end of the eighteenth century, though they still retained a fitted appearance for a decade or so, and knee-breeches were not completely outmoded for some time. There is an engraving of Captain Barclay, 'the celebrated pedestrian', dated c. 1820, which shows trousers worn as a feature of walking costume.

p. 30

what Camden has asserted: William Camden, the celebrated antiquarian (1551–1623), published the first edition of his *Britannia* in 1586; it is a topographical survey of the British Isles written in Latin. His *Remaines* was published in 1605, and the first volume of his *Annales* (an account of the reign of Queen Elizabeth) appeared in 1615. The reference to the shepherds occurs in his description of Merionethshire, where he quotes from Giraldus Cambrensis's *Itinerary Through Wales* of 1188, but Edward Lhuyd, the celebrated seventeenth-century scholar who translated Camden's descriptions of the Welsh counties for Edmund Gibson's edition of 1695 and expanded the Elizabethan's account, was sceptical: '. . . for mountains so high and their tops notwithstanding so near, that men may converse from them, and yet scarce be able to meet in a whole day; I presume there are none such in nature: and am certain there are not any in Wales, but men conversing from tops, may meet in half an hour.' (*op. cit.*, col 657).

The pass of Penman Mawr: the safe road traversing Penmaenmawr which Hucks speaks of was constructed in 1772, to the profound relief of Dr. Johnson who, travelling in Wales in the summer of 1774, speaks in his journal of 'a way, lately made, very easy and very safe. It was cut smooth and inclosed between parallel walls. The outer of which secures the [traveller] from the precipice which is deep and dreadful'. *The Yale Edition of the Works of Samuel Johnson*, ed. A. T. Hazen and J. H. Mitzendorf, 9 vols, New Haven, 1958–71, I. *Diaries, Prayers, and Annals*, ed. E. L. McAdam Jr., 1958, pp. 199–200).

We rose early etc.: for evidence that Hucks may not have made the ascent personally or that another member of the party may have been absent, see *Itinerary*, pp.109–10 below.

water was an article which we searched for in vain: cf. *The Rime of*

81

the Ancient Mariner, lines 119–122, 157–166. For a possible source of line 164 'Gramercy! they for joy did grin', see *Introduction*, pp.lxiv–lxv.

p. 31

The parched-up soldier of Alexander's army: in September 325 B.C. Alexander the Great set out from Patala on the Indus in N.W. India to reach Pura in Gedrosia; this involved marching inland from Ras Malan across the Mekran desert into what is now Baluchistan. Here his troops suffered greatly from thirst as a result of the dust and heat.

the sacred silence of his solitary reign: cf. Gray's *Elegy Written in a Country Church Yard*, line 12: 'Molest her ancient solitary Reign'.

some banditti, more terrible in aspect than ever Salvator Rosa could have painted: Salvator Rosa (1615–1673), the influential Neapolitan landscape painter, whose work like that of Claude and Poussin contributed to the eighteenth-century cult of the 'picturesque', specialized in depicting the more savage and rugged aspects of natural scenery. A leading art critic writes that '. . . many of his landscapes have their skies dark and laden, storms twist and turn the trees, melancholy lies over the crags and cliffs, buildings crumble into ruins, and banditti linger waiting for their prey . . .' (Rudolf Witkower, *Art and Architecture in Italy 1600—1750*, Pelican History of Art, Harmondsworth, 1958, p.216.) See, for example, the painting in the National Gallery known as 'Landscape with Figures' (No. 1206) once attributed to Rosa, though now considered to be a pastiche of his work. Cf. Richard Payne Knight, *The Landscape* (1794), I. 87–8:

> 'Or when, Salvator, from thy daring hand
> Appears, in burnish'd arms, some savage band.'

p. 34

the expedient of Ulysses: Odysseus (Roman Ulysses), the hero of Homer's *Odyssey*, filled his companions' ears with wax and had himself lashed to the mast of his ship, in order to withstand the alluring songs of the Sirens.

Abber Conway: Hucks is confusing Aber (or Llanaber) near Bangor with Aberconway, an alternative name for Conway (now Conwy).

the clergyman of the place: the Rev. Hugh Davies, B.A. was appointed Rector of Aber on 6 November 1787. (See A. I. Pryce, *The Diocese of Bangor During Three Centuries*, Cardiff, 1929, p.41.) Educated at Jesus College, Oxford, Davies was a distinguished botanist, a Fellow of the Linnaean Society from 1790, and highly esteemed by Thomas Pennant, whom he accompanied to the Isle of Man in 1774 and 1775. Master of his old school at Beaumaris for a time, Davies published a botany of Anglesey; he retired in 1818, and died at Baumaris in 1821, aged 81. (Information from R. R. Hughes, *A Biographical Epitome of Bangor Diocesan Clergy*, typescript Library of University College, Bangor, 1932).

p. 35 *shivering with cold*: this is the first intimation in the work of the party suffering from the effects of adverse weather conditions. Hucks's later allusions to a sore throat (p.43) and to catching cold (pp.47, 54) may not give substance to the family tradition that the seeds of his consumption were sown through over-exerting himself on the Welsh tour, but they do suggest that he was prone to such ailments for much of his life. (See *Introduction*, pp.xix, xxv above)

The first Edward: Edward I in fact built a pontoon bridge across the Menai Straits during the late summer and autumn of 1282, but the first troops to cross were ambushed and forced back by the Welsh, many of them being drowned. However, the bridge was used until the following summer to bring troops within striking distance of Caernarfon. (See *The History of the King's Works*, 1963, I. 354–7).
the actions of Alexander the Great: although Alexander III of Macedon (356–323 B.C.) made several famous river crossings, Hucks presumably has his legendary conquests chiefly in mind when comparing him to Edward I.
the insolent Xerxes: Xerxes I of Persia (c. 519–465 B.C.) built a bridge of boats across the Hellespont during his war with Greece.

p. 36 *another of king Edward's castles*: Beaumaris was the last and most advanced of Edward's North Walian castles, being built between 1295 and C. 1330 to guard the Menai Straits; never completely finished, it was allowed to decay, and saw little serious warfare.

the account given by Tacitus: Hucks here quotes from the *Annales*, Book XIV. 30.

p. 38 *the conquest of Peru and Mexico*: the Spanish under Hernando Cortes conquered central Mexico between 1519–21, and Francisco Pizarro led the conquest of Peru, 1532–5.
the taking of the island of St. Domingo: Santo Domingo was the name sometimes given to the island of Hispaniola in the West Indies, although during the colonial period the name belonged strictly to the Spanish portion alone. The island is now shared by the Dominican Republic and Haiti. Columbus discovered it in 1492, and subsequent Spanish settlers treated the Indian natives with great cruelty. In his *Poems* (1798) (p. 27) Hucks alludes to the reduction of the native population, according to William Robertson's *History of America*, from at least one million to sixty thousand in fifteen years:

Far in the western deep, from yonder isle
What tears and groans, what tortures and despair!
What horrid carnage dies the ensanguin'd plains!
What flames of war arise? what deeds of death!
(*The Retrospect*, lines 46–9).
that disgraceful and abominable traffic: at the time Hucks wrote,

83

the slave trade was still being pursued from British ports, a bill to prevent British merchants from supplying foreign settlements with slaves being carried in the Commons but defeated by the House of Lords in 1794. Slavery was not finally abolished in England until March 1807.

some old stones: Henry Rowlands in his *Mona Antiqua Restaurata* (1723), suggested that cairns and the cap-stones of cromlechs found on Anglesey were remains of Druid altars.

p. 39

Caesar in Gall, Lib. 6: Caesar's *Gallic Wars*, Book VI.

according to Tacitus: *Annales* XIV. 30.

p. 40

Acheron: one of the rivers of Hades in classical mythology. Hucks may, however, be thinking of Lake Avernus.

Gwyndn: Gwyndy, near Llynfaes, Anglesey. The name literally means 'white house', and might by extension actually be translated 'blessed place' (i.e. of hospitality).

p. 41

St. Kybi: St. Cybi (c. 550), possibly of Cornish stock, said to have been a cousin of St. David of Wales, founded a monastic community at Holyhead (Caer Gybi), which continued in existence into the sixteenth century. Several Welsh and two Cornish churches are named after him.

post multa pericula: 'after many dangers'.

Hoel Don Ferry: a misprint for Moel Don (now Moel-y-Don), as Hucks's list of towns makes clear. (p.73). For the suggestion that the party may have passed straight on to Caernarfon, see the *Itinerary*, p.110.

Caernarvon, or Caer-ar-fon: the town actually derives its name from *y gaer yn afon* 'the fort in the district of Arfon'.

p. 42

'Vast as the pride of its founder': Dr. Johnson in 1774 had been similarly impressed: '. . . . an Edifice of stupendous magnitude and strength . . . I did not think there had been such buildings. It surpassed my Ideas.' (*op cit.*, pp.203–4). Caernarfon Castle dates from 1283–1327, Edward's castle being built on the site of a Norman motte and bailey, later occupied by Welsh princes. It was perhaps the most important of the Edwardian castles, and the most substantial.

their future prince: it is often stated that the future Edward II, born at Caernarfon, was presented when a baby to the Welsh as their own native prince either at Caernarfon or at Rhuddlan Castle in 1284, but the story is unfounded; Edward was only made Prince of Wales at Lincoln in 1301.

p. 43

we made a party of three: there is no direct evidence as to the constitution of the party, but it would appear to have consisted of Hucks, Coleridge, and the 'skilled botanist', though there is no record that Brooke or Berdmore qualified for such a description (see note to p.29).

a luminous appearance: cf. *The Rime of the Ancient Mariner*, lines 264–73.

> Beyond the shadow of the ship
> I watch'd the water-snakes:
> They mov'd in tracks of shining white;
> And when they rear'd, the elfish light
> Fell off in hoary flakes.
>
> Within the shadow of the ship
> I watch'd their rich attire:
> Blue, glossy green, and velvet black,
> They coil'd and swam; and every track
> Was a flash of golden fire.

(see *Introduction*, p.lxv).

Phlegethon: a river in the classical underworld, in whose channel flames ran, instead of water.

a sore throat: cf. note to p.35 above.

Llyngwennyn bridge: presumably at Betws Garmon.

p. 44 *a fine lake*: Llyn Cwellyn.
another smaller one: Llyn-y-Cadair.

Traweth Mawr: several thousand acres of potential agricultural land on Traeth Mawr (the Great Sand) were successfully reclaimed in 1811 from the sea, which filled it every high tide. The project was inspired by William Alexander Madocks (1773–1828), founder of Tremadoc and Portmadoc. (See Elizabeth Beazley, *Madocks and the Wonder of Wales*, London, 1967).

p. 45 *'lodgings on the cold ground'*: 'My lodging is on the cold ground' is a song which occurs in Act V of Sir William Davenant's play *The Rivalls* (published 1668), where it is sung by Celania; the part was played by Mary Davis who subsequently became mistress to Charles II. Samuel Pepys saw the play on 10 September 1664; its first performance was probably in 1662. (We owe this information to Dr. David W. Lindsay.)

an old Welsh dictionary: probably Thomas Richards's *Antiquae Linguae Britannicae Thesaurus* (1753), although John Davies's *Antiquae Britannicae . . . Dictionarium Duplex* (1632) or Thomas Jones's *Welsh and English Dictionary* (1688) is also possible. (We owe this information to Professor Bedwyr Lewis Jones.)

Brutus in his tent at Philippi: cf. *Julius Caesar* IV. 3.

'pelting of the pityless storm': cf. *King Lear* III. 4. 29.

p. 46 *'And when rude blust'ring winds'*: cf. Collins's *Ode to Evening*, lines 33–36. Hucks is no doubt quoting from memory here, since the printed version runs:

> But when chill blust'ring Winds, or driving Rain,
> Forbid my willing Feet, be mine the Hut,
> That from the Mountain's Side,
> Views Wilds and swelling Floods . . .

p. 47   *the Druryd*: Afon Dwyryd.

p. 48   *man was not made for solitude*: cf. Cowper, *The Task* (1785), I. 248–9:

> If solitude make scant the means of life,
> Society for me!

the Cynfael: Rhaidr Cynfal.

p. 49   *an unexpected event obliges me to be at Bath*: there is nothing in Hucks's correspondence or that of the Gibbs family to suggest what this event might have been.

'tin sarcenick': 'dim saesneg' meaning 'I don't speak English'.

an extensive vale, or marsh: Morfa Harlech.

p. 50   *Harlech castle*: the castle was built by Edward I between 1283 and 1290; it is superbly situated overlooking Tremadoc Bay. It was captured by Owain Glyndŵr in 1404 and remained his capital for three years. It was the last North Wales castle to hold out (until 1468) for the Lancastrians in the Wars of the Roses, and for the Royalists in the Civil War, surrendering in 1647.

coup-de-main: the military term for a suprise attack.

p. 51   *the Golden Lion*: The Rev. Richard Warner spent a night at the Golden Lion in the summer of 1797, but complains of fleas and of 'being nearly suffocated by the closeness of a room nine feet by five and a half' (*op. cit.*, p.101).

p. 52   *a dark/Illimitable ocean* . . . etc.: *Paradise Lost*, II. 891–4.

p. 53   *Towen Merioinith*: Tywyn.

p. 54   *some fine remains of a castle*: Aberystwyth Castle was built c. 1277–89 above the river Ystwyth: a mint was established there during the Civil War. It was captured and slighted in 1646.

p. 55   *THE OLD PASSAGE*: the Beachley-Aust Ferry across the Severn. Another ferry, known as New Passage, though probably of equal antiquity, ran lower downstream from Black Rock to Chiswell Pill.

Llanindovrey: Llandovery.

p. 56   *Ragland castle*: Raglan Castle is a fifteenth-century structure, much of it the work of Sir William ap Thomas, 'the Blue Knight of Gwent'. It was slighted after a ten-week siege in 1646.

p. 57   *the abbey*: Tintern Abbey lies beside the main road between Chepstow and Monmouth; it was founded in 1131 for Cistercian monks, and was almost completely rebuilt in the thirteenth and fourteenth centuries. It was disestablished in 1536. William Wordsworth paid his first visit to the region in the summer of 1793 while on his way to stay in the Vale of Clwyd with his friend Robert Jones.

p. 58   *Persfield*: Piercefield Park, now the site of Chepstow racecourse, was a favourite tourist attraction towards the end of the eighteenth century; its magnificent landscaped grounds above the Wye were largely developed by Valentine Morris (d. 1789) who lavished much of his large fortune on them. His eventual insolvency forced him to leave England, and he became Governor of St. Vincent. The beauties of Piercefield are discussed in Thomas Whateley's *Observations on Modern Gardening Illustrated by Descriptions* (1770), and in William Gilpin's *Observations on the River Wye* (1782).

it has a castle: Chepstow Castle was built at various dates between 1067 and 1300, the original Norman structure being extended by William Marshal, Earl of Pembroke, and Roger Bigod III, Early of Norfolk. During the Civil War, it was held for the king and twice besieged, eventually being taken by Parliamentary forces.

p. 60   *a couple of stanzas from Churchyard*: see note to p.21 above. Hucks quotes from stanzas 6 and 7 of the opening of *The Worthiness of Wales*, though the punctuation is not that of Thomas Evans's 1776 reprint.

p. 61   *manes*: spirit (Latin).

a cat-call: a shrill piercing whistle, or the instrument used to produce this sound, frequently in theatres and concert-halls.

p. 62   *Adam Smith's Wealth of Nations*: Adam Smith, the celebrated Scottish political economist (1723–90), published *An Inquiry into the Nature and Cause of the Wealth of Nations* in 1776.

p. 63   *the final subjugation of Wales*: Edward I won his final victory over Llywelyn ap Gruffyd in 1282, and the latter's subsequent death ended Welsh hopes of a united and independent country.

p. 64   *Attica*: the area of Southern Greece in which Athens is situated. Much of the soil is unsuitable for growing corn, although olives, figs, and grapes thrive.

the great Czar Peter: Peter the Great of Russia (1672–1725) carried out far-reaching reforms, adopting many European customs and techniques to modernize his country culturally and economically.

the pompous descriptions of Young: Arthur Young (1741–1820) was the author of *A Six Weeks Tour Through the Southern Counties of England and Wales* (1768); *A Six Months Tour Through the North of England* (1770); *The Farmer's Tour Through the East of England* (1771). *A Tour in Ireland* (1780), and *Travels in France* (1792) followed.

the diffuse and voluminous work of Pennant: Thomas Pennant (1726–98) the most celebrated of the Welsh travel writers of his day, published Volume I of his *Tour in Wales* in 1778, a second volume appearing in 1784. He was an antiquarian, geologist, and zoologist, his *British Zoology* being published between 1761 and 1767.

p. 66

Krekith: Criccieth.
Pulhely: Pwllheli.
Llanrost: Llanrwst.
Caerwis: Caerwys.
Harleigh: Harlech.

p. 67

The land tax a few years ago: A new tax, later repealed, had been granted by Parliament on houses, land, tithes etc. as a war measure in 1692, property was valued and the Government took a variable proportion of the annual value. As time elapsed, the tax became mainly confined to landed property; it was made perpetual in 1797.

p. 69

the Macclesfield company: possibly Messrs. Roe and Co., of whom Pennant speaks in connection with the copper mines on Parys mountain, near Amlwch. (see p.40 above.)

the falls of the Caen and Morthway: Pistyll y Cain and Rhaeadr Mawddach.

according to Pennant: see Pennant, op cit., II. 165–6.

the pool of Three Grains: Llyn y Tri Greyenyn, actually 'the Lake of the Three Pebbles', at the head of the Talyllyn Pass.

p. 70

'a bidding'. O.E.D. gives 1810 for its earliest citation of 'bidding' as meaning an invitation or summons.

Conwyl: Cynwyl Elfed, Dyfed, formerly Carmarthenshire. Hucks's route would not have taken him within its vicinity, and it is interesting to speculate on the means by which the quoted document came into his hands.

p. 72

Llanvilling: Llanfyllin.
Llangunnog: Llangynog.
The Druid House: now Druid, near Corwen.
Llangollin: Llangollen.
Rudland: Rhuddlan.

p. 73

Gwyndn: Gwyndy, near Llynfaes.

Towen Merionith: now Tywyn, Gwynedd, formerly Merioneth-shire.
Pont ar Finach: Pontarfynach (Devil's Bridge).
Llanindovery: Llandovery.
Brecknock: now Brecon.

Coleridge's Letters Written on the Tour of Wales

(The definitive texts of Coleridge's letters are found in *The Collected Letters of S. T. Coleridge*, ed. E. L. Griggs, Oxford, 1956–71.)

1
TO ROBERT SOUTHEY

Stamped: Gloucester.

July 6th-[1794]. Sunday Morn. Gloucester
When you write, direct to me to be left at the Post Office, Wrexham, Denbighshire N. Wales. I mention this circumstance *now*, lest carried away by a flood of confluent ideas I should forget it.—You are averse to Gratitudinarian Flourishes—else would I talk about hospitality, attentions &c &c—however as I must not thank you, I will thank my Stars.[1] Verily, Southey—I like not Oxford nor the inhabitants of it—I would say, thou art a Nightingale among Owls—but thou art so songless and heavy towards night, that I will rather liken thee to the Matin Lark—thy *Nest* is in a blighted Cornfield, where the sleepy Poppy nods it's red-cowled head, and the weak-eyed Mole plies his dark work—but thy soaring is even unto heaven.—Or let me add (for my Appetite for Similies is truly canine at this moment) that as the Italian Nobles their new-fashioned Doors, so thou dost make the adamantine Gate of Democracy turn on it's golden Hinges to most sweet Music.

Our Journeying has been intolerably fatiguing from the heat and whiteness of the Roads—and the un*hedged* country presents nothing but *stone*-fences dreary to the Eye and scorching to the touch—But we shall soon be in Wales.

Gloucester is a nothing-to-be-said-about Town—the Women have almost all of them sharp Noses. As we walked last night on the Severn Banks, a most lovely Girl glided along in a Boat—there were at least 30 naked men bathing—she seemed mighty unconcerned—and they addressing her with not the most courtly gallantry, she snatched the Task of Repartee from her Brother who was in the Boat with her, and abused them with great perseverance &

1. Coleridge and Hucks were in Oxford from c. 16 June to 5 July, when they set off for Wales. During that time they were constantly in touch with Southey.

elocution. I stared—for she was elegantly dressed—and not a Prostitute. Doubtless, the citadel of her chastity is so impregnably strong, that it needs not the ornamental Out-works of Modesty.[1]

It is *wrong*, Southey! for a little Girl with a half-famished sickly Baby in her arms to put her head in at the window of an Inn—'Pray give me a bit of Bread and Meat'! from a Party dining on Lamb, Green Pease, & Sallad—Why?? Because it is *impertinent* & *obtrusive*—I am a Gentleman!—and wherefore should the clamorous Voice of Woe *intrude* upon mine Ear!?[2]

My companion is a Man of cultivated, tho' not vigorous, understanding—his feelings are all on the side of humanity—yet such are the unfeeling Remarks, which the lingering Remains of Aristocracy occasionally prompt. When the pure System of Pantocracy[3] shall have aspheterized [i.e. rendered common] the Bounties of Nature, these things will not be so—! I trust, you admire the word 'aspheterized' from *a* non, σφέτερος proprius! We really *wanted* such a word—instead of travelling along the circuitous, dusty, beaten high-Road of Diction you thus cut across the soft, green pathless Field of Novelty!—Similies forever! Hurra! I have bought a little Blank Book, and portable Ink horn—as I journey onward, I ever and anon pluck the wild Flowers of Poesy—'inhale their odours awhile'[4]—then throw them away and think no more of them—I will not do so!—Two lines of mine—

> And o'er the Sky's unclouded blue
> The sultry Heat suffus'd a *brassy* hue.

—The Cockatrice is a foul Dragon with a *crown* on it's head. The Eastern Nations believe it to be hatched by a Viper on a *Cock's* Egg. Southey.—Dost thou not see Wisdom in her *Coan*[5] Vest of Allegory? The Cockatrice is emblematic of Monarchy–a *monster* generated by *Ingratitude* on *Absurdity*. When Serpents *sting*, the only Remedy is—to *kill* the *Serpent*, and *besmear* the *Wound* with the *Fat*. Would you desire better *Sympathy*?—

Description of Heat from a Poem I am manufacturing—the Title 'Perspiration, a Travelling Eclogue [']6

1. Cf. Coleridge's use of the same phrase, in a later letter, p.102 below.
2. Cf. Mark Akenside, *The Pleasures of Imagination* (1744), II. 763–5:
   'I am a King,
   And wherefore should the clamorous voice of woe
   Intrude upon mine ear?'
3. Later the term had become 'Pantisocracy'. (See p. 97 below).
4. Unidentified.
5. A Coleridgean coinage for 'co-existing', 'double'?
6. *Poetical Works*, I. 56.

The Dust flies smothering, as on clatt'ring Wheels
Loath'd Aristocracy careers along.
The distant Track quick vibrates to the Eye,
And white and dazzling undulates with heat.
Where scorching to th' unwary Traveller's touch
The stone-fence flings it's narrow Slip of Shade,
Or where the worn sides of the chalky Road
Yield their scant excavations (sultry Grots!)
Emblem of languid Patience, we behold
The fleecy Files faint-ruminating lie.—

Farewell, sturdy Republican! Write me concerning Burnet[1] &
thyself and concerning &c &c—My next shall be a more sober &
chastised Epistle—but you see I was in the humour for
Metaphors—and to tell thee the Truth, I have so often serious
reasons to quarrel with my Inclination, that I do not chuse to
contradict it for Trifles.—To Lovell,[2] Fraternity & civic Remembrances. Hucks' Compliments!

S. T. Coleridge

2
TO ROBERT SOUTHEY

Stamped: Denbigh.

Wrexham. Sunday July 13th [1794]

Your Letter, Southey! made me melancholy. Man is a bundle of
Habits: but of all Habits the Habit of Despondence is the most
pernicious to Virtue & Happiness. I once shipwrecked my frail bark
on that rock—a friendly plank was vouchsafed me. Be you wise by my
experience—and receive unhurt the Flower, which I have climbed
Precipices to pluck. Consider the high advantages, which you
possess in so eminent a degree—Health, Strength of Mind, and
confirmed *Habits* of strict Morality. Beyond all doubt, by the
creative powers of your Genius you might supply whatever the stern
Simplicity of Republican Wants could require—Is there no possibility of procuring the office of Clerk in a Compting House? A
month's application would qualify you for it. For God's sake

---

1. George Burnett (1776?–1811) was a Somerset man and like Southey, a student at
   Balliol College, Oxford. He subsequently became a dissenting minister, an army
   surgeon, and a tutor in Poland. In 1807 he edited *Specimens of English Prose*.
2. Robert Lovell, (1770?–96), a Quaker poet from Bristol, was married to Mary
   Fricker, and was one of the original Pantisocrats; in 1795 he became Coleridge's
   brother-in-law. He died of a fever in April 1796.

93

Southey! enter not into the church. Concerning Allen[1] I say little—but I feel anguish at times.—This earnestness of remonstrance—I will not offend you by asking your Pardon for it! The following is a *Fact*—A Friend of Hucks's after long struggles between Principle and *Interest* (as it is improperly called) accepted a place under Government—he took the Oaths—shuddered—went home and threw himself in an Agony out of a two pair of stairs' Window![2] These *dreams* of Despair are most soothing to the Imagination—I well know it. We shroud ourselves 'in the mantle of Distress, And tell our poor Hearts, This is *Happiness*!['] There is a *dignity* in all these solitary emotions, that flatters the pride of our Nature. Enough of sermonizing. As I was meditating on the capabilities of Pleasure in a mind like your's I unwarily fell into Poetry

> 'Tis thine with faery forms to talk,
> And thine the philosophic walk,
> And (what to thee the sweetest are)
> The setting Sun, the Evening Star,
> The tints, that live along the sky,
> And Moon, that meets thy raptur'd eye,
> Where grateful oft the big drops start—
> Dear silent Pleasures of the Heart!
> But if thou pour one votive Lay,
> For humble Independence pray,
> Whom (sages say) in days of yore
> Meek Competence to Wisdom bore.
> So shall thy little Vessel glide
> With a fair Breeze adown the Tide—
> Till Death shall close thy tranquil eye
> While Faith exclaims 'Thou shalt not die![']³

'The heart-smile glowing on his aged Cheek Mild as decaying Light of Summer's eve'—are lines eminently beautiful. The whole is pleasing—.For a motto! Surely my Memory has suffered an epileptic fit. A Greek Motto would be pedantic—These Lines will perhaps do.

> All mournful to the pensive Sage's eye
> The Monuments of human Glory lie:
> Fall'n Palaces crushed by the ruthless haste

1. Robert Allen, a friend of Coleridge's at Christ's Hospital and an undergraduate at University College, Oxford, had recently introduced Coleridge to Southey in Oxford.
2. There is no record of whom this unfortunate friend of Hucks might have been.
3. An adapted version of lines 80–105 of Coleridge's poem *Happiness* (*Poetical Works*, I. 32)

Of Time, and many an Empire's silent waste
But where a Sight shall shuddering Sorrow find
Sad as the ruins of the human mind?[1]

                                        Bowles

A Better will soon occur to me—

Poor Poland! They go on sadly there.[2]

Warmth of particular Friendship does not imply absorption.[3] The nearer you approach the Sun, the more intense are his Rays—yet what distant corner of the System do they not cheer and vivify? The ardour of private Attachments makes Philanthropy a necessary *habit* of the Soul. I love my *Friend*—such as *he* is, all mankind are or *might be!* The deduction is evident.—Philanthropy (and indeed every other Virtue) is a thing of *Concretion*—Some home-born Feeling is the *center* of the Ball, that, rolling on thro' Life collects and assimilates every congenial Affection. These thoughts the latter part of your letter suggested.

What did you mean by H. has '*my understanding*[']? I have puzzled myself in vain to discover the import of the sentence. The only sense it *seemed* to bear was so like *mock-humility* that I scolded myself for the momentary supposition.—

My heart is so heavy at present, that I will defer the finishing of this letter till to morrow—I saw a face at Wrexham Church this morning, which recalled 'thoughts full of bitterness' and images too dearly loved![4]—'Now past and but remembered like sweet sounds of Yesterday!'[']5—At Ross (16 miles from Gloucester) we took up our quarters at the King's Arms, once the House of Kyrle,[6] the M. of R. [Man of Ross] I gave the window-shutter the following Effusion.[7]

> Richer than Misers o'er their countless hoards,
> Nobler than Kings or king-polluted Lords,
> Here dwelt the man of Ross! O Trav'ler, hear!
> Departed Merit claims the glistening Tear.
> Friend to the friendless, to the sick Man Health

1. Lines taken from William Lisle Bowles's poem, *The Philanthropic Society*, the last couplet later being used by Southey as the epigraph for his *Botany Bay Eclogues* (1797).
2. Poland was at this time in the grip of Kosciuszko's patriotic insurrection against the Russians, whose forces, supported by Prussia, had taken Cracow, and were besieging Warsaw.
3. See *Introduction*, p. xvi above.
4. See pp. 96–7, 101 below.
5. Quoted from William Lisle Bowles's sonnet 'Associations', Lines 4–5.
6. John Kyrle. See notes to p. 76 above.
7. *Poetical Works*, I. 57.

With gen'rous joy he view'd his modest wealth.
He heard the Widow's heav'n-breath'd prayer of Praise,
He mark'd the shelter'd Orphan's tearful gaze—
And o'er the dowried Maiden's glowing cheek
Bade bridal love suffuse it's blushes meek
If 'neath this roof thy wine-cheer'd moments pass,
Fill to the good man's name one grateful glass!
To higher zest shall Memory wake thy Soul,
And Virtue mingle in the sparkling Bowl.
But if, like me, thro' Life's distressful Scene
Lonely and sad thy Pilgrimage hath been;
And if, thy breast with heartsick anguish fraught
Thou journeyest onward tempest-tost in thought—
Here cheat thy cares—in generous Visions melt—
And *dream* of Goodness, thou hast never felt.

I will resume the pen to morrow.—

Monday 11 o'clock. Well—praised be God! here I am—videlicet—Ruthin, 16 miles from Wrexham.—At Wrexham Church I glanced upon the face of a Miss E. Evans, a young Lady with [whom] I had been in habits of fraternal correspondence—She turned excessively pale—she thought it my Ghost, I suppose—I retreated with all possible speed to our Inn—there as I was standing at the window passed by Eliza Evans, and with her to my utter surprize her Sister, Mary Evans[1]—quam efflictim et perdite amabam, [whom I loved madly and hopelessly]. I apprehend, she is come from London on a visit to her Grandmother, with whom Eliza lives. I turned sick, and all but fainted away!—The two Sisters, as H. informs me, passed by the window anxiously, several times afterwards—but I had retired—

Vivit sed mihi non vivit—nova forte marita
Ah dolor! alterius cara a cervice pependit.
Vos, malefida valete accensae Insomnia mentis,
Littora amata, valete! Vale ah! formosa Maria![2]

My fortitude would not have supported me, had I recognized her—I mean, *appeared* to do it!—I neither eat, or slept yesterday—but Love is a local Anguish—I am 16 miles distant, and am not half so miserable.—I must endeavor to forget it amid the terrible Graces of the wildwood scenery that surrounds me—I never durst

1. Coleridge was unhappily in love for several years with Mary Evans, the sister of a schoolfriend; her family lived in Villiers Street, off the Strand.
2. 'She lives, but not for me she lives: perhaps as an adored new bride-ah, misery!—she entwines about the neck of another. Farewell, you deceitful dreams of a mind aflame with love; beloved shores, farewell; farewell, ah, beautiful Mary!'

even in a whisper avow my passion, though I knew she loved me—Where were my Fortunes? And why should I make her miserable? Almighty God bless her—! her Image is in the sanctuary of my Heart, and never can it be torn away but with the strings that grapple it to Life.[1]—Southey! There are few men of whose delicacy I think so highly as to have written all this—I am glad, I have so deemed of you—We are soothed by communication—

Denbigh—8 miles from Ruthin.

And now to give you some little account of our journey—From Oxford to Gloucester, to Ross, to Hereford, to Leominster, to Bishop's castle, to Welsh Pool, to Llanvillin nothing occurred worthy notice except that at the last place I preached Pantisocracy and Aspheterism with so much success that two great huge Fellows, of Butcher like appearance, danced about the room in enthusiastic agitation—And one of them of his own accord called for a large Glass of Brandy, and drank it off to this, his own Toast—God save the King. And may he be the Last—Southey! Such men may be of use—they would *fell* the Golden Calf secundum Artem. From Llanvilling we penetrated into the interior [of] the Country to Llangunnog, a Village most roman[tica]lly situated—We dined there on hash'd Mutton, Cucumber, Bread & Cheese and Butter, and had two pots of Ale—The sum total of the expence 16 pence for both of us! From Llanvunnog we walked over the mountains to Bala—most sublimely terrible! It was scorchingly hot—I applied my mouth ever and anon to the side of the Rocks and sucked in draughts of Water cold as Ice, and clear as infant Diamonds in their embryo Dew! The rugged and stony Clefts are stupendous—and in winter must form Cataracts most astonishing—At this time of the year there is just water enough dashed down over them to 'soothe not disturb the pensive Traveller's Ear.[']² I slept by the side of one an hour & more. As we descended down the Mountain the Sun was reflected in the River that winded thro' the valley with insufferable Brightness—it rivalled the Sky. At Bala is nothing remarkable except a Lake of 11 miles in circumference.³ At the Inn I was sore afraid, that I had caught the Itch from a Welch Democrat, who was charmed with my sentiments: he grasped my hand with flesh-bruising Ardour—and I trembled, lest some discontented Citizens of the *animalcular*

1. Mary Evans eventually rejected Coleridge's suit in December 1794, to his great disappointment. In October 1795 he was married to Sara Fricker in Bristol, Southey marrying Sara's sister Edith the following month.
2. Unidentified.
3. Llyn Tegid.

Republic should have emigrated. Shortly after, into the same room a well drest clergyman and four others—among whom (the Landlady whispers me) was a Justice of Peace and the Doctor of the Parish—I was asked for a Gentleman [i.e. to propose a toast]—I gave General Washington.[1] The parson said in a low voice—(Republicans!)—After which the medical man said—damn Toasts! I gives a sentiment—May all Republicans be *gulloteen'd!*—Up starts the Welch Democrat—May all *Fools* be gulloteen'd—and then you will be the first! Thereon Rogue, Villain, Traitor flew thick in each other's faces as a hailstorm—This is nothing in Wales—they *make calling one another Liars &c*—necessary vent-holes to the sulphurous Fumes of the Temper! At last, I endeavored to arbitrate by observing that whatever might be our opinions in politics, the appearance of a Clergyman in the Company assured me, we were all *Christians*—tho' (continued I) it is rather difficult to reconcile the last Sentiment with the Spirit of Christianity. Pho!—quoth the Parson—Christianity! Why, we an't at Church now? Are we?—The Gemman's Sentiment was a very good one—'it shewed, he was *sincere* in his principles![']—Welch Politics could not prevail over Welch Hospitality—they all except the Parson shook me by the hand, and said I was an open hearted honest-speaking Fellow, tho' I was a bit of a Democrat.

From Bala we travelled onward to Llanvollin [Llangollen], a most beautiful Village in a most beautiful situation. On the Road we met the Cantabs of my College, Brooke[2] & Berdmore—these rival *pedestrians*, perfect *Powells*, were vigorously pursuing their tour—in a *post chaise!* We laughed famously—their only excuse was, that Berdmore had got *clapped*[3]—or else &c—From Llangollen to Wrexham, from Wrexham to Ruthin—to Denbigh. At Denbigh is a ruined Castle—it surpasses every thing I could have conceived—I wandered there an hour and a half last evening (this is Tuesday Morning). Two well drest young men were walking there—Come —says one—I'll play my flute—'twill be romantic! Bless thee for the thought, Man of Genius & Sensibility! I exclaimed—and preattuned my heartstring to tremulous emotion. He sat adown (the moon just peering) amid the most awful part of the

---

1. See the letter to Martin where Coleridge claims that he proposed the health of Joseph Priestley. (See *Introduction*, p. lxi)
2. E. L. Griggs adds an 's' to this name to conform to Coleridge's usage in Letter 3, but it does not appear to be needed. For brief biographies of Brooke and Berdmore, see note to pp. 80–1 above.
3. Coleridge presumably alleges that Berdmore was suffering from the effects of venereal disease, or is the term to be equated with the modern 'clapped out', exhausted? (But cf. p. 109 below.)

Ruins—and—romantic Youth! struck up the affecting Tune of *Mrs Casey*'—'Tis fact upon my Honor!

God bless you—Southey! We shall be at Aberistwith this day week—when will you come out to meet us—there you must direct your letter. Hucks' compliments—I anticipate much accession of Republicanism from Lovell! I have positively done nothing but dream of the System of no Property every step of the Way since I left you—till last Sunday.

Heigho!—

No signature in manuscript.

3

TO HENRY MARTIN[1]

Postmark: 25 July 1794. *Stamped* Caernarvon.

July 22nd 1794

Dear Martin

From Oxford to Gloucester x, to Ross x, to Hereford, to Leominster x, to Bishop's castle x, to Montgomery, to Welchpool, Llanvilling x, Llangunnog, Bala x, Druid House x, Llangollin, Wrexham xx, Ruthin, Denbigh x, St. Asaph, Holywell x, Rudland [Rhuddlan], Abergeley x, Aberconway x, Abber x over a ferry to Beaumaris (Anglesea) x Amlock [Amlwch] x, Copper mines, Gwindu, Moel don over a ferry to Caernarvon have I journeyed, now philosophizing with Hucks, now melancholizing by myself, or else indulging those day-dreams of Fancy, that make realities more gloomy. To whatever place I have affixed the mark x, there we slept. The first part of our Tour was intensely hot—the roads white and dazzling seemed to undulate with heat—and the country bare and unhedged presented nothing but stone-fences dreary to the Eye and scorching to the Touch—At Ross we took up our Quarters at the King's Arms, once the House of Mr Kyrle, the celebrated Man of Ross—I gave the Window shutter a few Verses, which I shall add to the end of the letter—The walk from Llangunnog to Bala over the mountains was most wild and romantic—there are immense and rugged Clefts in the mountains; which in winter must form Cataracts most tremendous—now there is just enough sun-glittering water

---

1. Henry Martin of Jesus College, who became successively the rector of parishes in Warwickshire and Somerset, finally becoming the incumbent of his native parish of. Silton, Dorset. Coleridge dedicated his first printed book, *The Fall of Robespierre*, published in September 1794 to him, this 'historic drama' being a joint production by himself and Southey.

dashed down over them to soothe, not to disturb the Ear. I climbed up a precipice, on which was a large Thorn-tree, and slept by the side of one of them near two hours. At Bala I was apprehensive, that I had caught the Itch from a Welch Democrat, who was charmed with my Sentiments—he bruised my hand with a grasp of ardor, and I trembled, lest some discontented Citizens of the *Animalcular* Republic might have emigrated. Shortly after, in came a Clergyman well drest, and with him 4 other Gentlemen—I was asked for a public Character—I gave, Dr. Priestley.[1]—the Clergyman whispered his Neighbour who it seems, is the Apothecary of the Parish—(Republicans!)—Accordingly when the *Doctor* (as they call apothecaries) was to have given a name, 'I gives a sentiment, Gemmen! May all Republicans be *gul*loteen'd!['] Up starts the Democrat 'May all Fools be gulloteen'd—and then you will be first!['}—Fool, Rogue, Traitor, Liar &c flew in each other's faces in hailstorms of Vociferation. This is nothing in Wales—they *make* it—: necessary vent-holes for the sulphureous Fumes of their Temper! I endeavoured to calm the Tempest by observing 'that however different our Political Opinions might be, the appearance of a Clergyman in the Company assured me, that we were all *Christians*—though I found it rather difficult to reconcile the last sentiment with the spirit of Christianity.' 'Pho.' quoth the Clergyman! 'Christianity! Why an't at *Church* now—are we? The Gemman's Sentiment was a very good one, because it shews him to be *sincere* in his principles.'—Welch Politics could not however prevail over Welch Hospitality—they all shook hands with me, (except the Parson) and said, I was an open-speaking, honest-hearted Fellow, tho' I was a *bit* of a Democrat.—On our Road from Bala to Druid House we met Brookes [sic] and Berdmore—our rival *Pedestrians*, a Gemini of *Powells*, were vigorously marching onward—in a postchaise! Berdmore had been *ill*. We were not a little glad to see each other. Llangollin is a village most romantically situated—but the Weather was so intensely hot, that we saw only what was to be admired—we could not admire.—At Wrexham the Tower is most magnificent—and in the Church is a white marble monument of Lady Middleton superior meâ quidem sententiâ [in my opinion

1. Joseph Priestley (1733–1804), dissenting minister, theologian, discoverer of oxygen, and revolutionary sympathizer, had embarked for the United States on 7 April 1794, following the burning of his Birmingham church, house and laboratory by an outraged mob in 1791 and three unhappy years in London. Coleridge wrote a sonnet as a tribute to Priestley (*Poetical Works*, I. 81), and praised him in *Religious Musings*, lines 371–6.

certainly] to any thing in Westminster Abbey.[1] It had entirely escaped my Memory, that Wrexham was the residence of a Miss E. Evans, a young Lady with whom in happier days I had been in habits of fraternal correspondence—she lives with her Grandmother—As I was standing at the Window of the Inn she passed by, and with her to my utter Astonishment her Sister, Mary Evans[2]—quam efflictim et perdite amabam—yea, even to Anguish—.They both started—and gave a short cry—almost a faint shriek—I sickened and well nigh fainted—but instantly retired. Had I appeared to recognize her, my Fortitude would not have supported me

> Vivit, sed mihi non vivit—nova forte marita
> Ah dolor! alterius carâ a cervice pependit.
> Vos, malefida valete accensae insomnia Mentis,
> Littora amata, valete! Vale ah! formosa Maria![3]

Hucks informed me, that the two Sisters walked by the Window 4 or 5 times, as if anxiously—Doubtless, they think themselves deceived by some Face strikingly like me—God bless her! Her Image is in the Sanctuary of my Bosom—and never can it be torn from thence but with the strings that grapple my heart to Life.—This circumstance made me quite ill—I had been wandering among the wild-wood scenery and terrible graces of the Welch mountains to wear away, not to revive, the Images of the Past! But Love is a local Anguish—I am 50 miles distant, and am not half so miserable.—At Denbigh is the finest ruined Castle in the Kingdom—it surpassed every thing, I could have conceived. I wandered there two hours in a still Evening, feeding upon melancholy.—Two well drest young Men were roaming there—'I will play my Flute here'—said the first—'it will have a *romantic* effect'. Bless thee, Man of Genius and Sensibility! I silently exclaimed. He sate down amid the most awful part of the Ruins—the Moon just began to make her Rays predominant over the lingering Daylight—I preattuned my feelings to Emotion—and the Romantic Youth instantly *struck up* the sadly-pleasing Tune of Mrs. Casey!

> The British Lion is my Sign—
> A Roaring Trade I drive on &c.—

Three miles from Denbigh on the Road to St. Asaph is a fine Bridge with *one Arch*—of great grandeur—stand at a little distance,

---

1. Coleridge undoubtedly refers to Roubiliac's monument to Mary Myddleton who died 8 April 1747. It depicts the Resurrection and stands on the north side of the chancel.
2. See note 1, p. 96 above.
3. See note 2, p. 96 above.

and *through* it you see the woods waving on the *Hill-bank* of the River in a most lovely point of view. A *beautiful* prospect is always more picturesque, when seen at some little distance thro' an Arch. I have frequently thought of Mich. Taylor's[1] way of viewing a Landscape by putting his head between his Thighs.—Under the arch was the most perfect Echo, I ever heard. Hucks sung, 'Sweet Echo'[2] with great effect. At Holywell I bathed in the famous St. Winifred's Well—it is an excellent cold Bath—at Rudland is a fine ruined Castle—Abergeley is a large Village on the Sea Coast—Walking on the sea sands—I was surprized to see a number of fine Women bathing promiscuously with men and boys—*perfectly* naked! Doubtless, the citadels of their Chastity are so impregnably strong, that they need not the ornamental Outworks of Modesty.[3] But seriously speaking, where sexual Distinctions are least observed, Men & women live together in the greatest purity. Concealment sets the Imagination a working, and, as it were, *cantharidizes* our desires.

Just before I quitted Cambridge I met a countryman with a strange Walking Stick, 5 feet in length—I eagerly bought it—and a most faithful servant it has proved to me. My sudden affection for it has mellowed into settled Friendship. On the morning of our leaving Abergeley just before our final departure I looked for my Stick, in the place where I had left it over night—It was gone—! I alarumed the House—No one knew anything of it—In the flurry of anxiety I sent for the cryer of the Town—and gave him the following to cry about the town and on the beach—which he did with a gravity for which I am indebted to his stupidity.

Missing from the Bee Inn, Abergeley—A curious Walking-Stick. On one side it displays the head of an Eagle, the Eyes of which represent rising Suns, and the Ears Turkish Crescents. On the other side is the portrait of the Owner in Wood-work. Beneath the head of the Eagle is a Welch Wig—and around the neck of the Stick is a Queen Elizabeth's Ruff in Tin. All adown it waves the Line of Beauty in very ugly Carving. If any Gentleman (or Lady) has fallen in love with the above-described Stick & secretly carried off the same, he (or she) is hereby earnestly admonished to conquer a Passion, the continuance of which must prove fatal to his (or her) Honesty; and if the said Stick has slipped into such Gentleman's (or Lady's) hand thro' Inadvertence, he (or she) is required to rectify the

---

1. Possibly the English politician Michael Angelo Taylor (1757–1834), M.P. for a number of constituencies including Poole and the city of Durham between 1790 and 1834.
2. Presumably the Lady's Song from Milton's *Comus* (lines 230–43).
3. Cf. p. 92 above.

mistake with all convenient Speed.—God save the King.

Abergeley is a fashionable Welch Watering Place—and so singular a proclamation excited no small crowd on the Beach—among the rest a lame old Gentleman, in whose hands was descried my dear Stick. The old Gent. who lodged at our Inn, felt great confusion, and walked homewards, the solemn Cryer before him, and a various Cavalcade behind him. I kept the Muscles of my Face in tolerable Subjection. He made his lameness an apology for borrowing my Stick, supposed he should have returned before I had wanted it &c—Thus it ended except that a very handsome young Lady put her head out of a Coach Window, and begged my permission to have the Bill, which I had delivered to the Cryer. I acceded to the request with a compliment, that lighted up a blush on her Cheek, and a Smile on her Lip.

We passed over a ferry and landed at Aberconway—We had scarcely left the Boat ere we descried Brookes[sic] & Berdmore, with whom we have joined Parties, nor do we mean to separate.—Our Tour thro' Anglesea to Caernarvon has been repaid by scarcely one object worth seeing. To morrow we visit Snowdon—&c—Brookes, Berdmore and myself at the imminent hazard of our Lives scaled the very Summit of Penmaenmawr—it was a most dreadful expedition! I will give you the account in some future Letter.

I sent for Bowles's Works, while at Oxford[1]—how was I shocked—Every Omission and every alteration disgusts Taste & mangles Sensibility. Surely some Oxford Toad has been squatting at the Poet's Ear, and spitting into it the cold Venom of Dullness. It is not Bowles—He is still the same (the added Poems prove it)—descriptive, dignified, tender, sublime. The Sonnets added are exquisite—Abbe Thule has marked Beauties—and the Little Poem at Southampton is a Diamond—in whatever light you place it, it reflects beauty and splendor. The 'Shakespeare' is sadly unequal to the rest—yet in whose Poems, except in those of Bowles, would it not have been excellent?[2]

Direct to me, my dear Fellow!—to be left at the Post Office, Bristol—and tell me everything about yourself, how you have spent the Vacation &c—

---

1. Presumably William Lisle Bowles, *Sonnets, With Other Poems*, Third edn., Bath and London, 1794; Coleridge developed a youthful admiration for Bowles's work, and Hucks paraphrases lines from 'Monody, Written in Matlock' in the *Tour* (see note to page 25).

2. On the Guildhall Library transcript of this letter, William Lisle Bowles has written indicating his pleasure at Coleridge's praise, and explaining the adverse comments.

believe me, with gratitude and fraternal friendship
            Your obliged
                    S. T. Coleridge

Lines written at Ross, at the King's Arms—once the House of Mr. Kyrle.

Richer than Misers o'er their countless hoards,
Nobler than Kings or king-polluted Lords,
Here dwelt the Man of Ross! O Stranger,[1] hear!
Departed Merit claims the glistening tear.
If 'neath this Roof thy wine-cheer'd moments pass,
Fill to the good man's name, one grateful glass.
To higher Zest shall Memory wake thy soul,
And Virtue mingle in th' ennobled Bowl.
But if, like me, thro' Life's distressful Sc[ene]
Lonely and sad thy Pilgrimage hath be[en;]
And if, thy Breast with heart-sick angu[ish fraught,]
Thou journeyest onward tempest-tost in[thought;]
Here cheat thy cares; in generous Visio[ns melt,]
And *dream* of Goodness, thou hast never *felt*.

The faded Flower.[2]

Ungrateful He, who pluck'd thee from thy stalk,
Poor faded Flowret! on his careless way;
Inhaled awhile thy odours on his walk,
Then onward pass'd and left thee to decay.
Ah melancholy Emblem! had *I* seen
Thy modest Beauties dew'd with evening's Ge[m,]
I had not rudely cropt thy parent stem;
But left thee blushing 'mid the enliven'd Green.
And now I bend me o'er thy wither'd Bloom,
And drop the tear—as Fancy at my Side
Deep-sighing points the fair frail Abra's Tomb,[3]
'Like thine, sad Flower! was that poor Wanderer's pride!
'O lost to Love & Truth! whose selfish Joy
'Tasted her vernal sweets—but tasted to destroy!'

Of course B and B [i.e. Brooke and Berdmore] desire their kind remembrances.

1. Cf. *Poetical Works* I. 57. The reading 'O Stranger' is not noted.
2. Another version of this sonnet appeared in *Poems*, by Robert Lovell and Robert Southey, Bath, 1795, p. 68, but neither Coleridge nor Southey printed the poem in later editions of his poetical works. However, E. H. Coleridge includes it in *Poetical Works*, I. 70.
3. The Southey version of 1795 has 'Emma's' for 'Abra's'. A transcription of this sonnet, dated 10 July 1794, initialled 'S.T.C.' and written in an unknown hand, is in the Pierpoint Morgan Library; in line 11 it also reads 'Emma's'.

Lines Addressed to S. T. Coleridge.

Whose are those sad complainings? From the vale
Of peace they come; in sorrow's wildest garb,
Fashion'd to deepest feeling: they are sounds
That on the world's cold ear unheeded die,
Heard, but not felt—for they can never claim
A brotherhood with joy—but yet my heart
That never has disclaim'd the kindred tear
Of sympathy, shall not disown it now.
My *Friend* has touch'd the Lyre, it's deep-ton'd strings
Swept by the hand of sorrow! I can sigh
(Cold tho' I am with the world's fellowship,
And much estrang'd) even at the common call
Of poor humanity; and can I joy,
When He, with whom I sojourn'd in the vale
Ere while of hope, in life's ingenuous hour,
When he, my earliest friend, has rais'd his voice
In grief?—Be friendship's holy call obey'd.

Oft in the lonely hour, when sadness steals
Upon the troubled thought, and cankering care
Sits heavy in the heart; in memory's stores,
I seek the med'cinable balm, and fly
(Even like the feather'd prisoner from it's cage,
Wild with new liberty) to those fair days
That saw us musing on the willowy banks
Of Granta's lazy stream; or journeying on,
Elate with youthful hope, o'er Cambrian wilds;
Toiling with weary feet, up the steep hill
Precipitous, o'er many a huge rough rock,
Or thro' the lengthening vale, or deep-worn glen,
Dark with impending woods; aye big with schemes
Air-built, of never-fading happinesss:
Wild dreams of folly in the vacant hour,
That once I fondly cherish'd—They are fled.
Oh! I had rais'd me up a building, fair
As in the morning, and to every eye
Lovely; but when the threshold I had reach'd,
Buoyant with hope; it vanish'd from my gaze
And left me comfortless: But that is past!
New scenes succeed, and other views arise,
Of this our playful being. Be it so.
And thus, my Friend! even of the bitter cup

I too with thee have tasted; but complaint
Is weakness;—to despair is sin.—The clouds
Heavy awhile may lower, and the dark storm
Upon the unfriended heads of those that weep,
Fall pitiless—there is a sky beyond,
Peaceful, and pure, unsullied with a cloud,
Where the tir'd pilgrims of the earth shall rest.

Deem not the friendships of your earliest days
False tho' 'chance-started;' haply yet untried,*
They are judg'd hardly; o'er the stormy world
Fate has dispers'd them wide; some too oppress'd
With sorrows, nameless load, drag on with pain
A being full of misery; or like thee,
Of friends most false complain.—I blush to think
That there are such. But cheerily I look
Forward to hours of social converse sweet,
In life's calm evening, circled with the friends
Of former days, when all it's harsher tints
Soften'd by time, the memory shall renew
Painless.
   Forgive me, Thou to whom these lines,
Artless and rude belong, if I have wak'd
One painful feeling; nor obtrusive deem,
What friendship dictates: 'tis the wish sincere,
That thou with changed eye, the varying forms
Should'st view of nature, and not always draw
The pensive moral, from her gloomiest hues;
That 'midst her walks of beauty thou should'st smile,
And in the scale of being view thy place
Not solitary, (and if right I judge

* A brief while,
Some have preserv'd me from life's pelting ills;
But like a tree with leaves of feeble stem,
If the clouds lasted, or a sudden breeze
Ruffled the boughs, they on my head at once
Dropt the collected show'r, and some most false,
False and fair-foliag'd as the manchineel,
Have tempted me to slumber in their shade,
Even 'mid the storm.

(Hucks is here quoting lines 20–28 of Coleridge's dedicatory poem 'To the Rev. George Coleridge', prefixed to his *Poems* of 1797, though the phrase 'chance-started' occurs at the beginning of line 20 where the poet speaks of himself as 'Chasing chance-started friendships'. Hucks's poem was almost certainly inspired by Coleridge's dedication and the implied slur on his friends which it contains. (See *Introduction*, pp. lxii–lxiii)

Of changeful chance in life's conflicting scenes)
Not yet unenvied. Pleasant are the paths,
And sweet the simple bowers, that in the vale
Of humble life, peace with no niggard hand,
And meek content have form'd: to them unknown,
The feverish hours, tumultuous hopes and fears,
The war of struggling passions, wan disease,
Inbred of Cities; pale disastrous want,
Wealth's feeble offspring; vice and fell remorse.
O never, never, may the sickly gale,
From life's infected prisons, o'er the fields
Rich with new harvests, and the plenteous grain,
Blow noxious, mildewing many a ripening ear!

Thrice happy He, who from the giddy whirl
Secluded, and the turmoil strange of life,
Dwells in the shade of peace! He not in vain
Upon his quiet path shall woo the charms
Of science, nor the hallow'd light implore
Of calm philosophy. The stars that gild
The brow of night, and thro' the Empyreal waste
Thick interwoven, seem no less than Heav'n!
The rolling Sun, the changeful moon and all,
Maker of worlds! that in thy goodliest works,
Displays thee WONDERFUL; shall raise his soul
To love and holiness, and more exalted hopes
Of that unknown HEREAFTER, that awaits
Our fearful going, from this narrow bourne.

The Itinerary

The attentive reader may become aware of some discrepancies with regard to dates between Hucks's account of the tour and that provided by Coleridge's letters printed in Appendix I. The last letter Coleridge wrote on the tour was apparently that to Henry Martin of 22 July 1794, in which he supplies a list of towns visited, indicating by a cross those in which the travellers spent the night; Hucks's book provides an itinerary too, together with the distances between towns, with asterisks to denote the number of nights slept in each. From a correlation of the two lists, together with the evidence of Coleridge's letters and the *Tour* itself, the facts which follow emerge.

1. The travellers are in almost total agreement concerning the events of the first fortnight of the tour (5–18 July):

5 July. From Oxford to Gloucester. Walk on Severn bank. Night at Gloucester.

6 July. Gloucester to Ross-on-Wye. S.T.C. writes first letter to Southey. Night at King's Arms, Ross.

7 July. Ross to Leominster. Night at Leominster.

8 July. Leominster to Bishop's Castle. Night at Bishop's Castle.

9 July. Bishop's Castle to Llanfyllin. S.T.C. 'preaches Pantisocracy'. Night at Llanfyllin.

10 July. Llanfyllin to Bala. Dinner at Llangynog. Quarrel at inn at Bala. Night at Bala.

11 July. Bala to Druid [House]. J. H. writes [?] Letter I. Leave Bala late—meet Brooke and Berdmore in a post-chaise. Night at Druid.

12 July. Druid to Wrexham. Welsh harper at Llangollen. Night at Wrexham.

13 July. Day in Wrexham. S.T.C. sees Mary Evans, begins second letter to Southey. Night at Wrexham.

14 July. Wrexham to Denbigh. Dinner at Ruthin. J.H. begins [?] Letter II. Denbigh Castle by moonlight. S.T.C. continues letter to Southey. Night at Denbigh.

15 July. Denbigh to Holywell. J.H. finishes Letter II. S.T.C. finishes letter to Southey. Bridge on road to St. Asaph commented on. S.T.C. bathes at Holywell. Night at Holywell.

16 July. Holywell to Abergele. Rhuddlan Castle. J.H. bathes at Abergele. J.H. begins [?] Letter III (dated 'Abber 16

108

July'—did he mean Abergele, or Aberconwy (Conwy), or Aber? If not the former, he must have mistaken the date). Night at Abergele.

17 July. Abergele to Conwy. S.T.C. loses stick. Reappearance of Brooke and Berdmore at Conwy; J.H. visits church. Night at Conwy.

18 July. Conwy to Aber. Party now consists of J.H., S.T.C., Brooke, and Berdmore. Arrive at Aber late in evening. Night at Aber.

2. After 18 July the rival accounts are contradictory until Coleridge's evidence ceases with his letter to Martin of 22 July. The main point at issue is the length of stay at Aber: Hucks's table claims that the party spent two nights there (presumably 18 and 19 July), while Coleridge's letter to Martin only allocates one night (18 July) to Aber before the crossing to Beaumaris. However, both writers assert that members of the party climbed Penmaenmawr; if Coleridge's account is to be believed, it would seem that the day-long ascent of the mountain (19 July) was followed the same evening by the crossing to Anglesey. Hucks however affirms that the expedition up Penmaenmawr occupied the party for much longer than its members anticipated, that they descended at dusk, and did not gain the inn at Aber until about nine o'clock, spending the evening discussing their experiences (see p. 31 above). Thus it would seem likely that the party *did* spend two nights at Aber, contrary to Coleridge's account, crossing to Beaumaris on Anglesey during the evening of 20 July. There is still one further curious fact to be noted: Coleridge's letter to Martin of 22 July includes only Brooke, Berdmore, and himself in the party which scaled Penmaenmawr, making a point it would seem of omitting Hucks's name. One may assume that Coleridge could hardly have been mistaken as to the composition of the party or Hucks's absence from it, and thus Hucks's account of the climb, despite its apparent authenticity, may in fact have derived from his companion's reminiscences, Hucks on this occasion speaking of himself, not, as he promises in the preface, 'as being the only spectator', but as the spectator of events he did not even witness! This conjecture would lead one to question the accuracy of the remainder of his account at sundry points, but of course it may have been Coleridge who was in error. We know that when the quartet first encountered one another on the road from Bala, Berdmore had been ill (see p. 100 above); was *he* the member who stayed behind in Aber while the others climbed Penmaenmawr? We also know from Hucks's fifth letter that he declined to ascend

Snowdon later in the tour because of a cold, but Coleridge can hardly have muddled the two climbs (and thus omitted Hucks from the wrong one), since the journey to Snowdon was not undertaken until the day following the letter.

Whatever the true answer, the problem stresses the importance of not relying unduly on either *A Pedestrian Tour* or Coleridge's letters as unimpeachable accounts of what occurred on the tour. If we accept Coleridge, the following itinerary emerges:

19 July. Aber to Beaumaris. Brooke, Berdmore, S.T.C. climb Penmaenmawr in daylight. Cross by ferry to Beaumaris in evening. Night at Beaumaris.

20 July. Beaumaris to Amlwch. Party cross Anglesey, and spend night at Amlwch.

21 July. Amlwch to Caernarfon. The copper mines, Gwyndy, Moel-y-Don ferry to mainland. Night at Caernarfon.

22 July. Caernarfon to Beddgellert. S.T.C. writes to Martin 'Tomorrow we visit Snowdon'. Journey to Beddgellert. Night in hut near Snowdon.

Hucks's list and account provide an alternative picture:

19 July. Day at Aber. J.H., S.T.C., Brooke, and Berdmore climb Penmaenmawr, not returning to inn till 9 p.m. Evening spent discussing day's events. Night at Aber.

20 July. Aber-Beaumaris. Visit to falls at Aber? J.H. completes Letter III. Crossing by ferry to Beaumaris in evening. Night in Beaumaris. (In Hucks's list Beaumaris is not asterisked, but the Tour (p. 35) makes it clear that the travellers spent a night at the inn there).

21 July. Beaumaris to Amlwch. Night at Amlwch.

22 July. Amlwch to Moel-y-Don. The copper mines, dinner at Gwyndy, arrive at Moel-y-Don ferrry. Night at Moel-y-Don.

23 July. Moel-y-Don to Caernarfon. J.H. begins [?] Letter IV, dated from Caernarfon, *19* July. (This must be wrongly dated; even Coleridge does not suggest that the travellers arrived in the town before the evening of 21st). J.H.'s remark 'We crossed the ferry yesterday morning' (i.e. 23rd) suggests however that his letter was continued on 24th. Night at Caernarfon.

Thus there is uncertainty as to the date of both crossings, to and from Anglesey, and as to where the party spent the nights of 19th, 20th, 21st and 22nd July.

110

3. Coleridge's letter of 22 July from Caernarfon is his last extant piece of writing from the Welsh tour, and thereafter we have no independent witness as to the accuracy of Hucks's record; the strange fact is, however, that the datings of Hucks's Letter V from Tan-y-Bwlch on 24 July, of Letter VI from Aberystwyth on 29th, and of Letter VII from the Old Passage on 2 August are only viable if *Coleridge's* itinerary and dating of the earlier part of the tour are adhered to! If the party *did* arrive at Caernarfon on 21st rather than 23rd July, and made the journey to Beddgellert on 22nd rather than 24th, then the pedestrians could have been at Tan-y-Bwlch on 24th after sleeping two nights in or near Beddgellert, just as Hucks's list claims. The details would then read:

23 July. At Beddgellert. Ascent of Snowdon by Brooke, Berdmore, and S.T.C. Night at Beddgellert.

24 July. Beddgellert to Tan-y-Bwlch. J.H. begins [?] Letter V. Night at Tan-y-Bwlch.

25 July. At Tan-y-Bwlch. Visit to Rhaeadr Cynfal and Rhaeadr Du. Night at Tan-y-Bwlch.

26 July. Tan-y-Bwlch to Dolgellau via Hariech and Barmouth. (I believe J.H.'s list to be in error here, and that the party did *not* sleep in Barmouth). Night at Dolgellau.

27 July. Dolgellau to Tywyn [Towyn]. Ascent of Cader Idris. Night at Tywyn.

28 July. Tywyn to the Aberdovey ferry. Night at the ferry.

29 July. Aberdovey Ferry to Aberystwyth. J.H. writes [?] Letter VI. Night at Aberystwyth.

30 July. Aberystwyth to Tregaron. Night at Tregaron.

31 July. Tregaron to Llandovery. Night at Llandovery.

1 Aug. J.H. parts company from others, and walks from Llandovery to Abergavenny.

2 Aug. J. H. walks from Abergavenny to the Old Passage. Writes [?] Letter VII. Night at the Old Passage.

3 Aug. J.H. crosses to the Bristol shore. Walks to Bristol. (His account ends here, but it allows the best part of two days for him to walk the seventy-five miles or so from Bristol to Exeter, in order to arrive, as Mrs. Hucks's journal states on 4 August. According to the *Tour* (p. 49 above), he had business in Bath, which would also have to be transacted during this period, unless he returned home first. He may not have *walked* from Bristol to Exeter, of course, but possibly transacted his business in Bath on 3 August, and then made his way home by coach or on

111

horseback. At all events, the sequence above, based on Coleridge's dating of the middle portion of the tour, does make a coherent whole.

4. On the other hand, it is difficult to refute Hucks's own account in the *Tour* of nights spent at comfortable or incommodious inns, of places visited and sights seen. If we accept the evidence of the *Tour*, we must assemble the following diary of events:

24 July. Caernarfon to Beddgellert. J.H. finishes Letter IV. The party spend the night in a hut near Snowdon.

25 July. Brooke, Berdmore and S.T.C. ascend Snowdon, while J.H. returns to the inn. The climbers descend about 4 p.m. Night at Beddgellert.

26 July. Beddgellert to Tan-y-Bwlch. The party reach Tan-y-Bwlch in the evening. (J.H. begins [?] Letter V, misdating it 24 July). Night at Tan-y-Bwlch.

27 July. Day at Tan-y-Bwlch. Visit to Rhaeadr Cynfal and Rhaeadr Du. The party plant to leave Tan-y-Bwlch 'tomorrow'. Night at Tan-y-Bwlch. (J.H.'s third asterisk is thus wrong).

28 July. Tan-y-Bwlch to Dolgellau. Pass through Barmouth (J.H.'s asterisk is wrong—he does not *mention* a night there). Night at Dolgellau.

29 July. Dolgellau to Tywyn [Towyn]. Ascent of Cader Idris. Night at Tywyn—damp sheets episode.

30 July. Tywyn to ferry near Aberdovey. Night at the 'solitary house' near the ferry.

31 July. To Aberystwyth early in the morning. J.H. writes [?] Letter VI, dating it 29 July. (J.H. gives Aberystwyth an asterisk, but since the party arrived there early in the morning, and he does not mention a night there in the text, it seems likely they went on to Tregaron the same day). Night at Tregaron.

1 Aug. Tregaron to Llandovery. Night at Llandovery. (J.H. does not mention this in the text of the *Tour*, but his list stars it).

2 Aug. J.H. parts company with others, and journeys on from Llandovery via Brecon and Crickhowell to Abergavenny. Night at Abergavenny. (Again he does not mention sleeping there, but his list stars it).

3 Aug. J.H. walks from Abergavenny to the Old Passage. Detained by the weather, he writes [?] Letter VII, misdating it 2 August. Night at the Old Passage.

112

4 Aug. J.H. crosses ferry at the Old Passage, and walks to Bristol, then possibly on to Bath to attend to his business. If he really reached home on 4 August, as Mrs. Hucks's journal suggests, then he must have resorted to a speedier form of transport for the last part of his journey from Bath or Bristol to Exwick, though if we are to satisfy Mrs. Hucks's statement that he walked 700 miles the 629 miles of Hucks's itinerary must be supplemented with the distance between Bath or Bristol and Exeter.

Thus it is impossible finally to establish where Hucks and his fellow-travellers were, or what they did, on any given day after 18 July from the mutually-contradictory accounts before us. We know that Hucks apparently modified the travellers' participation in the ideological quarrel at the inn in Bala, (see pp. lxi and 14–15 above) according to Coleridge's account—or was Coleridge laying claim to a republican bravado he never exhibited? Conversely, when Hucks claims to have made the perilous ascent of Penmaenmawr where Coleridge excludes him, was he pretending to feats of athleticism he never performed? It seems unlikely, in that he was prepared to describe his actions in print, and at least three men who knew the truth were capable of challenging his veracity. Did the party really spend a night in a 'miserable hut' at Moel-y-Don, or was Hucks merely adding a little piquant Welsh colour to an otherwise bald narrative? If not, why did Coleridge not include the night on the banks of the Menai Strait in his letter to Martin? Or did the mark of a cross beside the name Caernarfon in the letter in fact represent that uncomfortable night at Moel-y-Don, Coleridge not differentiating between one side of the Strait and the other?

These and other discrepancies serve to remind us that men's minds and memories are frequently fallible and inconsistent one with another, and especially so at an epoch and in a country where firm and accurate indications of time and date were not always readily available. Both Hucks and Coleridge were young undergraduates on holiday, anxious to see as much as possible, and often recording their impressions hurriedly and in diverse circumstances: undoubtedly a letter begun in a certain place on a certain day would be completed and dispatched at another time and place, and the writer would be unconcerned to render his use of 'yesterday' or 'tomorrow' consistent. Moreover, Hucks's original letters (if they really existed) may have borne little indication of place and date; when he came to edit them for publication and to prepare his list of towns visited, he had quite possibly forgotten the full details of his itinerary and the exact dates and places where he had sat down to write letters which allegedly were, after all, originally intended for 'the amusement of an individual' rather than for the enlightenment of posterity.

IRISH

BAY

CAERNARFON BAY

ANGLESEY SHIRE

CARNARVON

CARDIGAN BAY

MER

SH

CARDIG

— Sir WATKIN WILLIAMS WYNN Bar.ᵗ
This MAP of
NORTH WALES
Is respectfully inscribed
By his obliged and obedient Servant —
John Evans